Praise for

The Queen of My Self

"Finally, an archetype of midlife power and maturity that I can relate to—the Queen. Thank you Donna for providing this much-needed missing piece of women's wisdom."

> —Christiane Northrup, M.D., author of *Women's Bodies, Women's Wisdom* and *The Wisdom of Menopause*

"This is the book we've been waiting for—blunt, witty, truthful, intelligent, and downright astonishing in its lucidity. Donna Henes bravely paves the way for women through 'the Grand Canyon of midlife change.' For those intrepid ones among us who intend to take ownership of our lives no matter what, this book is our revolutionary manifesto."

> —Vicki Noble, co-creator of *Motherpeace Tarot* and author of *Shakti Woman* and *The Double Goddess*

"In *The Queen of My Self*, Mama Donna cooks up a nourishing stew of regal empowerment from a rich assortment of ingredients including rituals, blessings, and many stories from her life and practice. Flying in the face of our stereotypes, self-doubts, and cultural conditioning she offers an exuberant and elegant vision of midlife as a time of power, wisdom, beauty, and joy."

> —J. Ruth Gendler, author of *The Book of Qualities*

"Delightfully written, at once playful and profound, *The Queen of My Self* is a treasure! Donna Henes successfully weaves together the personal, the universal and the historical with candor and humor."

> —Cristina Biaggi, Ph.D., author of *Habitations of the Goddess* and *Footsteps of the Goddess*

The Queen
of
My Self:

STEPPING INTO SOVEREIGNTY IN MIDLIFE

DONNA HENES

MONARCH

Monarch Press
Brooklyn, New York

The Queen of My Self: Stepping into Sovereignty in Midlife
Copyright © 2005 by Donna Henes

Published by

MONARCH

Monarch Press
P.O. Box 380403
Brooklyn, NY 11238
www.thequeenofmyself.com

The Queen of My Self™, "Turn your midlife crisis into your crowning achievement"™, and The Queen Suggests™ are registered trademarks.

Library of Congress Cataloging-in-Publication Data
is available.

ISBN 978-0-9758906-0-8

9 8 7 6 5 4 3 2

Book design by Patricia Smith
Cover design by Greg Olear and Patricia Smith
Author photo by Trinh Thai

Printed in Canada
Second Printing 2007

All tribute to Daile
who has made so much possible for me.

Contents

Acknowledgments

To my fabulous agent and friend, Deirdre Mullane, who rescued the Queen and championed Her with inspired intelligence and unflagging enthusiasm.

To Patricia Smith, who came into my life and lifted me from the low tech, inefficient dark ages. May she be blessed for all her efforts on my behalf.

To Chrissie Rivera, Eve Katz, and Janice Pemberton, my magical right and left hand Jills of All Trades. Their help made it possible.

To Dr. Susan Corso and Daile Kaplan, who graciously offered generous material support to the Queen's Treasure Chest.

To the wonderful women in my life for their endless patience with my Queen-obsessed Self. Their insights, advice, encouragement, and practical support was invaluable. All thanks to Nancy Azara, Dianne Barnes, Cristina Biaggi, Stephanie Capparell, Rosemary Dudley, Carolyn McViker Edwards, Lois Guarino, Geraldine Hannon, Judyth Hill, Daile Kaplan, Willow LaMonte, Karen Malpede, Dominique Mazeaud, Sandi Miller, Judith Mullen, Linda Siegel, Sarah Teofanov, Kay Turner, Gail Wasserman, and Suzanne Zuckerman.

To my mother, Adelaide Trugman, a Queen before her time.

To all the organizers and participants in "The Queen of My Self™ Workshops" who so generously and eloquently shared their stories.

To the Omega Institute for their gift of grace and time in their Hermitage, affording me the uninterrupted luxury to think and write.

Foreword

Every woman who has reached midlife already knows that it is a struggle to create—and constantly recreate—your own self, your own myth. The task demands bravery, independence, the willingness to risk trusting yourself, and a capacity for joy. As important and empowering as the archetype of the Crone has become as a guide to this stage of our lives, many of us are rejecting Her as the sole model for middle-aged women today. Many a student of mine has had to endure my rants about the stifling and absurd limits of the "Crone."

Within reading the first few pages of the manuscript of *The Queen of My Self,* I had goose bumps: Donna Henes was on to something! Donna's ideas about aging will become an important part of the current dialogue and will inspire you to find your own ideas and your own way of taking control of your life and destiny. This book had to be written for all of us.

You may find that some of Donna's conclusions are the same as yours. I did. All women are on the front lines in our efforts to survive, care for others, have dignity, find meaning, and celebrate life. But it is easy—and awful—to feel like the only one. In our efforts to address issues of aging for ourselves and others, we can feel alone on that front line unless we see others doing the same: trying to both live and share our deepest beliefs, baring ourselves, with all the risks that implies.

Praise Goddess, Donna's doing all that, and she shows that all women are, or preparing to do the same as they enter midlife. We each add our own unique discoveries or perspectives to the dialogue, according to our own truths; shared insights help us find more of our own.

Women, you are Queens, blessed by the pollen of bees, filled with Gaia's power. Bare yourself to yourself. Then bare yourself to others. You are not alone. Read on.

—Francesca De Grandis, author of *Be a Goddess!* and *The Modern Goddess' Guide to Life*

On Finding Myself Middle-Aged

With No Role Model I Could Relate To

> *How do we get the life we want?*
> *I am a loosed boat floating*
> *a thousand miles.*
>
> —*Yu Xuanji, Chinese poet (843-868)*

A few years ago, the editor of the preeminent international magazine devoted to the female spirituality/goddess movement approached me to write an article for an upcoming issue on the subject of the Crone. The Crone, according to the popular mythic model of the three Stages of Womanhood, represents old age, the third and final period of a woman's life, following upon the stages of the young Maiden and the fertile Mother.

The editor was particularly interested in my holistic perspective and thirty years of experience as an urban shaman and contemporary ceremonialist specializing in celebrations of the cycles of the universe and the seasons of life, all informed by natural history and science as well as multicultural folklore and ritual practice. More to the point perhaps, as far as the topic of the Crone was concerned, she was aware that I am, as is she, a woman in my middle years. She knew that I, like millions of other women of my generation, was foundering in the extreme transitions—in turn disorienting, troubling, frightening, stimulating, and thrilling—that are brought about by menopause and other radical personal changes in midlife.

This profound transformation has traditionally marked the passage from the domesticated and care-taking Mothering stage of a woman's life—whether she has birthed and nurtured babies, careers, artistic creations, or all of the above—to that of the Crone, the wizened and wily old lady. The Crone is the ancient wise one, cultural repository and visionary counselor-in-residence, who dispenses Her profound sagacity with patience and largesse. This editor was sure that I, though in my mere early fifties and still bleeding, would automatically identify myself as a Crone.

But I balked. I was not then, nor am I now, a few years later, an old woman. Nor am I nearly so wise as I hope to be when I am truly a Crone of great age and incontrovertible knowledge. What's more, I am not planning on retiring from an active role in the world any time soon. It is entirely too early to rest on my laurels. I haven't finished planting them all yet. There is still so much to do, to see, to learn, to experience. And so precious little time. No, I am definitely not patient. Rather, I am raging with determination, suddenly all too aware of the tenure of my mortality.

While it was flattering that this editor had approached me, writing about the Crone seemed entirely too limiting. After all, I wanted a completely different identity, a more resonant role than the Crone for my own middle years. I kept feeling that there should be a newly defined continuum of Womanhood. I craved, but could not find, an existing prototype of a passionate and empowered female middle age. The writings of Jean Bolen, Joan Borysenko, Elizabeth Davis and Carol Leonard, Geraldine Hanon, and Christiane Northrup, among others, also expressed a desire for an expanded view of the old archetypes of the life cycle of women. Their words were an enticing foretelling of a generational imperative. A new archetype was definitely in the air, but I felt that it had not yet been completely articulated.

So, in the absence of a fully fleshed-out portrait of the aware, independent, attractive, and influential older woman of the world I aspired to be—once I made my way through the dizzying maze of menopause and emerged at the other end—I set out to invent one for myself. Was this hubris? Who was I to challenge such a powerful prototype? Well, I was, in fact, a proud member of the pioneering Sixties Generation, and consequently, I had a certain amount of experience in rebelling against the status quo of old archetypes and striving to replace them with new, more inclusive, and personally relevant ideals. Our generation has demonstrated time and again that it is possible to create our own characters, compose our own scripts, and author the sagas of our own lives. We are our own role models.

The mythic model that I came to envision is recognizably like me, like us. Not yet old, yet no longer young, She is a regal Queen standing in Her proper place—after the Mother and before the Crone in No Woman's Land. She plants Her flag and claims Her space in this previously uncharted midlife territory. Still active and sexy, vital with the enthusiasm and energy of youth, the Queen is tempered with the hard-earned experience and leavening attitudes of age. She has been forced to face and overcome obstacles and hard lessons, including Her own self-limiting tendencies, and in so doing has outgrown the boundaries of Her old self. Impatient with the inessential and restless for authenticity, She sheds all attachment to the opinions of others and accepts complete responsibility and control over Her life. She is the Queen of Her Self, the mature monarch, the sole sovereign of Her own life and destiny. Here, finally, is an archetype that fits.

As long as I live, I will have control over my being—you find the spirit of Caesar in me.
—Artemisia Gentileschi, Italian painter (1593-1652)

This book is an articulation of that vision of regal self-empowerment. Indeed, it is a result of that vision. When I first began conceptualizing the Queen, I literally dreamt of a ceremonial crowning. In this moving Crowning Ceremony, I ascended the throne of my passion and power and pledged my Self to myself. Always aware of the promise of that dramatic nocturnal ordination, I have worn my crown of self-confidence ever since. The more I think about the Queen, the more I become Her. And the more Queenly I become, the more I desire to be in the company of other Queens.

I hereby cordially invite you to join me on a royal expedition, a noble quest to discover meaning, moxie, and magic in midlife and beyond. This will not be a resort vacation, but a challenging and extraordinarily rewarding journey into the wilds of heretofore unmapped realms. Hiking shoes are definitely in order. This exhilarating adventure follows the twisting path that leads from confusion to actualization, from crisis to resolution, from doubt to resolve, from fear to fortitude, from lack of self-esteem to evolved, life-affirming spirited strength and self-determination. The Queen, supreme paradigm of mature female potency, will be our esteemed mentor and guide.

I offer my services as the advance scout. By way of orientation and interpretation, I contribute an itinerary based on my own experience in affirmative aging in the hopes that it will be inspiring and useful as we chart our course. *The Queen of My Self: Stepping into Sovereignty in Midlife* is not intended to be a precise roadmap, but rather, an "On the Road" journal written by a sister fellow traveler to titillate our spirit of adventure. There are no pat answers here, no set lists outlining and numbering the so-called sure and easy steps to happiness, fulfillment, enlightenment, and love. As I am sure you already know, there is nothing easy about this trip, and every woman must follow her own trail. The Queen, ever true to the process and power of exploration and discovery, declines to preach "How To." Rather, She impels, implores, "Why Not?" And "If not now, honey, *when?*"

The Queen teaches by example and also by metaphor. On these pages you will find the stories of women, mine included, throughout time and from many different societies, situations, and stations who have successfully crossed the hard divide and created daring and dynamic lives for themselves. These compelling her-stories are woven together with folklore, poetry, myth, practical suggestions, exercises, affirmations, celebrations, rituals, and invocations. Altogether they create a larger-than-life archetypal framework that helps us to elevate our personal aging process to legendary proportions. Here is a mythological mirror of our own midlife experience. When we look into its depths, we can see our own royal potential and the clear reflection of our own inner monarch.

The Queen paradigm promotes a new understanding of what it might mean to be a middle-aged woman today who accepts full responsibility for and to herself, and it celebrates the physical, mental, emotional, and spiritual rewards of doing so. Becoming a Queen is not automatic. The Queen bursts forth from adversity and previous constraints, actual or imagined, to become a proficient player in the game plan of Her choice. The Queen does not invite hard times and trouble, but She chooses to use them well. Actualized, organized, efficient, self-sufficient, competent, ethical, and fair, the Queen has struggled for and earned Her authority and respect. Determined and firmly centered on Her own two feet, She dares to climb, step after step, with nascent surety into the heady realm of Her own highest sovereignty.

Once ensconced upon Her throne, the Queen glows golden with confidence, competence, and grace. She is fully aroused and takes great pleasure in the feelings of freedom, elation, and well-being that come from personal empowerment. This thrilling post-menopausal period of vitality, renewed energy, enhanced self-esteem, optimism, and enthusiasm comes to us in direct proportion to the intensity of our own conscious engagement in the process and consequences of transformation. Another gift of self-enfranchisement is the potent and extremely liberating sexuality of the Queen. Shining from the inside out, Her attractiveness and attraction is rooted deeply in Her self-actualization, self-worth, and inner strength. She exudes a primal excitement, Her power palpable in Her very presence.

This new view of a strong, sexual, spirited, and successful middle-aged woman is becoming ever more visible in popular culture. The Queen's growing appeal is evident in the media, politics, advertising, and the arts. The massively influential energy of women now entering midlife has released our generational issues and standards out into society at large. By making our personal changes within the holistic context of a larger reality, we are transforming our cultural tastes and mores as we transform ourselves.

The Queen of My Self: Stepping into Sovereignty in Midlife encourages women to adapt the lessons we have learned, the experience we have gained, the victories we have achieved from our willingness and ability to grow, to effect a positive, humane, sustainable change for the greater good of all. It is my hope that as more and more women rise to reign in the fullest potential of our supremacy, we will harness our purpose, passion, and power and direct it toward creating a more balanced and peaceful world. This is the legacy of Her majesty.

Long Live the Queen!

Donna Henes
Exotic Brooklyn, New York
The New Sturgeon Moon

CHAPTER 1

Ladies in Waiting

TREADING WATER IN TURBULENT TIMES

*The old woman I shall become will be quite different
from the woman I am now. Another I is beginning,
and so far I have not had to complain of her.*

—George Sand, French writer (1804-1876)

As I anticipated my fiftieth birthday, I naturally assumed that I should have a special ceremony to mark a full half-century of life on Earth. Such a milestone clearly deserves a spectacular commemorative event, particularly since I am, by profession, a celebrationist. I have spent the better part of my adult life organizing and writing about auspicious occasions for all of life's seasons and transitions for individuals and the general public alike.

My first thought was that my own ritual should be a Croning Ceremony to honor the end of my tenure as a potentially fertile woman and my entry into the next phase of my life. Cronings are all the rage these days among women of my generation. Invitations and announcements pour in monthly from friends who choose to celebrate this major rite of passage, this scary fiftieth birthday, in a manner that honors the emotional and spiritual impact of its importance. My phone lines have been burning up with requests from midlife women who want me to guide them spiritually through this great transition from Mother to Crone.

But when it was my turn to mark this passage, a Croning Ceremony just didn't feel right. I was definitely not a Crone. The Crone archetype describes a woman in the third and final stage of her life who is an all-knowing, all-giving source of wisdom dispensed with steady grace. Serene in my wisdom, I was not. My body and emotions were flaming, my systems, my equilibrium, fluctuating madly. Too hot. Too cold. Too tired. Too anxious. Too sad. Too irritated. I was all over the place.

I hadn't slept eight hours in a row in eons. For months on end, my major aerobic activity had been my nightly wrestling match with my on-again, off-again covers. No one ever told me that a common associate of menopause is insomnia, not to mention headaches. No one ever told anyone anything. Menopause was a dirty little secret, never discussed. All I ever heard was that you stop bleeding and you go crazy. Well, no wonder. Constantly exhausted, I was overly sensitive, frazzled, scared, furious, rubbed raw by all this nerve-wracking upheaval. I was in the midst of a hugely profound change and I wasn't altogether sure of who I would be when the process was complete. I was a masterpiece-in-progress, but hardly the weathered old wise one.

My resistance was not born of fear of aging—especially considering the alternative. As Woody Allen put it, "I don't want to be immortal through my work. I want to be immortal through not dying." I have absolutely every intention of being a very, very old woman. Actually, I look forward to my tenure as a delightfully outrageous, brazenly courageous Crone, living her golden years to the hilt. And believe me, I practice daily to achieve that romantic and ambitious end. When I grow up to be a Crone, I want to be a Grandma Moses, a Mother Teresa, a Maria Sabina, a Martha Graham, a Georgia O'Keeffe, or a Delaney sister—a truly stellar elder whose visionary influence extends far into the future.

How could I, in all honesty and any modesty, claim the mantle of the Crone while a mere middle-ager? That would be like saying that someone who is in their twenties is as smart and as practiced as I am. What did I know of the enormity, the complexity of life compared to someone who has lived thirty, forty, fifty years longer than I? How many more births, deaths, tragedies, pleasant surprises, and simple twists of fate has an eighty-five-year-old woman witnessed, participated in, learned from? I was long past being a Maiden and I was no longer a Mother, but I was certainly not an old woman, either. I was a powerful woman coming into my prime. It seemed to me that an entire stage of life—*my* stage—was missing from the widely accepted mythological descriptions of the Three Ages of Womanhood.

THE ROLES OF A LIFETIME

My own Maidenhood, like that of many Baby Boomers, was a long one, lasting well into my thirties. My twenties and early thirties were characterized by intense bouts of physical activity, intellectual stimulation, emotional inquiry, spiritual search, geographical exploration, sexual experimentation, and creative engagement. I wanted to see, do, learn, experience, absolutely *everything*. Unmarried, and unfettered by convention, I was like the Goddess Diana, driven by a fearless curiosity through vast fields of experience, savoring my freedom and the succulence of life, sowing my wild oats.

Eventually, my Mother self kicked in and Mama Donna took over. I settled into a more sedentary, though very nontraditional, domestic existence and focused my energy on nesting, creating a home, and developing a spiritual center. For nearly a decade it really worked well. Life was idyllic, romantic, fun. I loved playing house and happy homemaker, nurturing my eclectic collection of loved ones. I had a loft that I was building around me like a snail shell. I had an extremely close community of friends who were my functional family. I had a foster son and his extended clan. I had a grownup-feeling love relationship. I had dogs and cats and birds and moths, a gold fish, and a praying mantis. I had my work, my writing, my ritual practice, my art. I was safe in the home sweet home zone and, in the words of Martha Washington, feeling "steady as a clock, busy as a bee, and cheerful as a cricket."

Then the shit hit the fan in my early forties, and my carefully constructed, well-cosseted world collapsed around me. For more than a decade, my life was defined and dictated by loss. In that space of time, I lost my home, my community, my livelihood, and several so-called friends who couldn't take the enormously debilitating pressures of my life. I lost my youth, my sense of security, my delusions of immortality, and my zest for living. Death and more death burrowed in around me. Both of my parents, my oldest dear friend, four more close friends, some women in my circles, and all three of my cats died, and my now-adult foster son was diagnosed with a deadly disease that sapped my strength and spirit, as well as his.

At one point during the tortuous times of my midlife transition, my astrologer friend remarked, "The universe has been squeezing you so tight for so long, that the extraordinary pressure will turn you into a diamond by the time you are in your fifties." Yeah, from a lump of coal. When my fiftieth birthday arrived, I was still dealing with the aftershock from that deluge of death and all of the other losses that I had suffered. Still mired in my muddy menstrual machinations, my physical and emotional changes held me in draining thrall. I was working hard to transform my aggregate grief and grow from the knowing of it. But while I toiled deep in the mines of my soul, it would be a few years yet before I would see the light on the other side of that terrible tunnel.

Although it has often felt like it over the years, I am not alone in my midlife passage. My story, albeit with a different script and cast of characters, is essentially the same as the herstory of each of the women of my generation who are now entering middle age. Though we are each on our own life journey, each traveling our own personal path of trial and error, trauma and tribulation, mastery and victory, we all face the universal certainty of age and change.

Search. Search. Seek. Seek.
Cold, Cold. Clear. Clear.
Sorrow. Sorrow.
Hot flashes. Sudden chills.
Stabbing pains. Slow agonies.
—Ching-Chao, Chinese poet (1084-1151)

THE CRISIS

Aging and changing might be inevitable, but it ain't easy. It precipitates in us a great uncertainty. The myriad dramatic disturbances of modern midlife—menopause, health concerns, career shifts, the empty nest, divorce, and death—create an overwhelming crisis of identity and purpose for each of us. What follows is an intense period of questioning absolutely everything—our goals and achievements, our priorities and our operating systems, our morals and our values, our fantasies and our fears. Some of us spend a considerable amount of time—easily ten or fifteen years—swirling in the turbulence of this middle age reassessment. Who are we supposed to be at this stage of our lives when we are less likely to be bound and identified by our kinship connection to someone else—as a daughter, a wife, a mother, a lover? What exactly is our role as older-than-young and younger-than-old women who are still active and more effective than ever?

This middling transitional shift into the next stage of our being promises us a vast world of positive possibilities for the second half of life. But first, before we are able to avail ourselves of the advantages and rewards of maturity, we must cross the Grand Canyon of midlife change, steep, rocky, and ripped asunder by a whole panoply of seismic ripples—mental, emotional, and spiritual—beyond the obvious physical ones. We climb and climb, and still we lose ground. The earth that we once trusted to be solid under our feet is slipping away and we are dragged out to sea, where we bob along in uncertain waters in a leaky boat with no map to guide us.

It seems as if
I'll never get beyond
the foot prints that I made.
—Qernertuq, Eskimo poet (c. 1200)

In her book *Goddesses in Older Women*, the therapist Dr. Jean Bolen writes that menopause is "a time of great spiritual and creative unfolding—although it sometimes feels like great unraveling." Unraveling, indeed. The whole damn sweater is falling apart and we are standing here naked in the cold (and we are *still* hot). Nothing has prepared us for this landslide of transitions that greets us as we enter our middle years. There we were, going along as always, then one day out of the blue, we discover ourselves to be middle-aged. Blindsided in a youth-conscious culture, we never saw it coming, but the overwhelming evidence of our aging can hardly be ignored.

The loss of our youth is probably most immediately evident in the changes to our bodies. We are beginning to experience the first signs of declining eyesight and hearing loss, as well as loss of inches in our height, pigment in our hair, strength in our muscles, mass in our bones, resiliency in our immune systems, and collagen in our skin. We suffer loss of sleep, loss of memory, and, as television advertisements mercilessly remind us, loss of perfect control of our bladders. Then there is the dispiriting loss of gravity, which unfortunately makes us the opposite of weightless. I remember when I was a child watching my grandmother getting dressed and staring at her pendulous breasts in horror, praying desperately that I wouldn't have *those things* when I was old.

Sometime, usually between about forty-five and fifty-five, we lose our monthly blood and hormonal balance. No matter how much we might have minded the fuss and muss of our periods, there is an alarming awareness of irrevocability when they stop. It is, after all, the end of a thirty- or forty-year way of being in the world. Menopause marks the termination of our participation in the bottom-line, bigger-than-we-are, biological imperative of our species. Our reproductive potential is now no longer an option. Whether or not we chose to use it when we had it is not the point. What is crucial is the feeling that our choices have narrowed.

Women of the Sixties Generation were the first to enjoy an unprecedented access to a variety of birth control methods. It was also largely the women of those politicized times who demanded, and ultimately won, the right to legally decide the destiny of our own bodies. Once in possession of this precious, personal choice of whether or not to become and/or stay pregnant, we have chosen, on the whole, to have fewer babies and at a more advanced age than ever before in history. Freed of what we considered to be biological tyranny and possessed of sophisticated ecological concern, fully one fifth of us chose not to have children at all.

As the tenure of our Mother time ends, it causes many of us to re-evaluate the choices that we have made about fertility, decisions that have defined our life for the past few decades. The finality of menopause really rankles. Some women who had never wanted babies now suddenly become nostalgic for what might have, could have, been. Recently, my friend Barbara, an art therapist and educator who is approaching her forty-ninth birthday, confided that she was thinking, for the very first time in her life, that maybe she wanted to have a child after all. Or not. Or maybe a divorce. Or *something*. Something was definitely missing, some lost chance, gnawing at her sense of certainty.

Thirty-three years after writing a ground-breaking piece in *Look* magazine about not wanting to have children, the writer Betty Rollin admitted not long ago on the pages of *Modern Maturity* that she was "one of those old-time 'career girls' who forgot to have children. At the age of sixty," she continued, "I began to mourn for the children I never had." Others, upon consideration, are secure and still satisfied with their earlier choice to remain childless, or what many in that category prefer to call childfree. One such woman wrote in response to Rollin's recent article that Rollin's earlier piece had been "a source of strength" over the decades to resist the social pressure to have children when she knew she didn't want them.

For the first time in history, large numbers of women of our generation, especially those with careers, deferred starting a family until we were in our late thirties and forties. Births to women between the ages of forty and forty-four increased seventy-one percent between 1990 and 1999. Now many of us are still very much occupied in the Mother mode when we reach our menopausal years. Our hormonal changes (a decline of estrogen and progesterone needed for reproduction and an increase of androgens that stimulate our assertiveness) produce a visceral withdrawal from and disinterest in mothering that is often at odds with the requirements of our parenting responsibilities. Our priority shifts from the desire to attend to the needs of others, to the imperative drive to address our own.

One woman in my Queen Workshop, a fifty-eight-year-old psychotherapist with a sixteen-year-old son, was extremely articulate about her conflicting emotions. Saundra told me that though she adores her child, there is just something primal, deep within her, that recoils at having to shower all of her nurturing attention on him when she is so desperately drawn to care for herself. "Where is your mother?" she teases him when she is most resentful (and, needless to say, extremely guilty about it). "It's not me, babe. No, no, no. It's not me you're looking for, babe."

Many others with children now face the future with an empty nest, our kids grown and off creating lives of their own, which leaves us with huge amounts of unaccustomed time to use as we please. This would be extremely liberating if it didn't also make us feel so lonely and insecure. I can't tell you how many times I have heard women exclaim in jubilation as their mothering days run out, "And now, it's my turn!"—the mantra of middle age. Then they stop in their tracks, dumbstruck, as they realize that they are now free to pursue their deferred dreams, they have no idea any more of what it is that they want for themselves.

After a couple of decades of serving the needs and desires of others, we have lost sight of our own. Our early aspirations were sacrificed on the altar of nurturing others, murdered by self-denial, dashed by adversity, and starved by neglect. Not only do we "lose" our children at this stage of life, we also lose our sense of Self. As Jacqueline Kennedy Onassis poignantly put it, "What is sad for women of my generation is that they weren't supposed to work if they had families. What were they going to do when the children are grown—watch the raindrops coming down the window pane?"

For the twenty percent of us who are not biological mothers, it is still extremely important to acknowledge that we have, in fact, been Mothers in the archetypal sense. We have been birthing careers, mothering social causes, nurturing creative endeavors, tending businesses, mentoring students and co-workers. If, as it has been said, "Some people give birth to children and some give birth to culture," then we were the Culture Mothers, the Mothers of Necessity, the Mothers of Invention. And it is all this that we have created and worked so hard to grow that we now stand to lose in one way or another. Whether career change is forced upon us or is the result of our own volition, there is still sure to be a transitional upheaval. Some women fear the loss of job security, others face imminent retirement, and still others take the bull by the horns and decide to leave and look for more satisfactory positions. For many midlife women, the proverbial glass ceiling prevents any further advancement up the corporate ladder.

Lois, a playwright I know, had been teaching in the theater department of a prestigious university for eleven years when, at the age of fifty-five, her bid for tenure was denied and she was let go. Her plays had been published widely, translated into several languages, produced by theater companies all over the world, and reviewed in major newspapers. She was a wonderful teacher who was well loved by her students, especially the young women who saw in her an admirable role model. What more could you ask for? But none of this mattered. It was simply cheaper to replace her with a younger, poorly paid adjunct. Lois's disappointment stung even more, coinciding as it did with her teenage daughter's adolescent hell, as well as her own menopausal disruptions.

Successful women who have made huge strides in the business world are now, in midlife, also reevaluating their life choices. Gail, a member of one of the Spirit Support Groups that I conduct, is the vice-president of a major auction house who curates international exhibitions, writes books, appears on television, and lectures around the country. A completely self-made woman, she was living an exciting, glamorous life that she hardly dared to imagine as a girl. At fifty-three, she found her career booming, and her life growing ever more busy and hectic, but rather than excite her as it once did, the pace simply made her tired. She was deeply dissatisfied and out of balance. "Don't get me wrong," she explained to me, "I was extremely proud of what I have accomplished in my life. But I was so focused on making money and moving up the ladder that I didn't even realize how much I was missing. I need to not work so hard and spend some energy on my emotional and spiritual side." Something lost, something gained.

Now, typically, by the time we have reached our middle years, our once-robust parents have begun to need more and more attention and care, too. Though certainly some people are orphaned early in life, while others who are in their seventies have at least one parent alive (I actually know three women my age or older who still have living grandparents!), most of us face the impending decline and ultimate death of our parents at about the same time as we are grieving the loss of our children, born and unborn. Many of us are compelled by circumstances to care for both parents and children at the same time, sandwiched, as it were, between the needs of the two generations, making the final years of motherhood the most difficult of all. For women without children, the realization that there will be no one to take care of us when we are old is one of the reasons that we may reconsider our status. Perhaps not the greatest motive for childbearing, but under the circumstances, a very understandable concern.

The extensive losses and pressures of midlife also often combine to place tremendous stress on our spousal relationships. While those of us who are married or living together are engaged in our midlife changes, our partners are experiencing changes of their own as we are each challenged to reexamine our choices and priorities. It is ironic that at a time in life when our world view naturally begins to broaden beyond our own prescribed lives, many of our world-weary spouses start to turn their attention away from the demands of their jobs and back toward home and family. Just when we are poised to abandon our role as keeper of the nest, our mates come flying home to roost.

The timing couldn't be more unfortunate. Now that we are trying to re-direct our focus onto our own intentions and goals, we have precious little patience left for any more claims on our time and attention. Our partner's sudden desire for more domestic intimacy seems stifling and needy. Many of us might agree with one woman who said, "Thinking about my husband's retirement, I realized I married him for better or for worse—not for lunch." Another friend complains that her husband calls her ten times a day at work. He rarely has anything to say, he just wants to hear her voice. "Where was he when we were younger and I wanted to spend as much time with him as possible?" she asks.

Our nerves are raw to begin with, so that the irritants in our marriages that we might have once considered to be minor and maybe even overlooked, now become completely overblown. No longer willing to hold our peace, hide our opinions, ignore our needs, placate our mates' feelings, or subjugate ourselves in any way whatsoever, we realize that ongoing disagreements once swept under the rug for the sake of peaceful coexistence or for the sake of the children, have now become intolerable. Deep-seated disagreements or major resentments that have remained unresolved over the years can drive us to distraction, if not to divorce.

And what of single, divorced, or widowed women? Every day we are showered with media messages extolling young love and sex, and ridiculing romance among the mature. While some have despaired at ever mating up, those of us who are seeking to be in a relationship with a man have been warned that we have a better chance of being in a terrorist attack (or is it struck by lightning?) than finding a husband after the age of forty. Others cringe at the notion of dating and physical intimacy, fearing to expose our menopausal bodies and mood swings. Of course, not all women want to be with men. Lesbians, being less bound to our culture's characterizations of aging, beauty, desirability, and appropriate feminine behavior, often have an easier time looking for love in middle age. Still others, women who are intently focused on our own immediate growth—perhaps for the first time ever—do not feel a need to be in any sort of love union at all, with our careers, studies, hobbies, travels, community work, friendships, and solitude fulfilling all of our immediate wants.

"These past couple of years have been very stressful for me," explained one woman who participated in a recent Queen Workshop. "My husband died of lung cancer two years ago. Four months later, I was forced to move because I could not afford the maintenance and mortgage on our home. A friend helped me to find a studio apartment, which meant that I had to downsize quite a lot and give away most of my old possessions, which was a painful task. But I was surprised to find that it helped me to focus on what was really important to me. For the first time in years, I was forced to reassess my priorities. In an odd way it was a relief to get rid of so much old stuff. Now I feel like I have room in my life for me. The bottom line is that now I am enjoying this time on my own to become reacquainted with myself, my spirituality, and my relationship to God."

The profound changes in the chemistry of our bodies and in our intimate relationships, the terrifying disruptions of our status quo, the daily life-and-death dramas we are forced to deal with, are incredibly disorienting. Not only are we burning up physically, blasted with flashes from our out-of-control internal furnaces, we are also, many of us, burnt out on an emotional level after years of tending the home, the hearth, and usually a job as well. Society tells us, and many of our own experiences have verified, that now that we are menopausal, we are poised to lose everything that has so far defined us: our power of reproductivity, our youth, our sex appeal, our children, our parents, our spouses, our time left on the job, our very visibility. This grim prognosis is frequently internalized by midlife women as loss of direction, motivation, enthusiasm, and self-esteem. Our fear, our grief, is expressed as confusion, depression, and furious rage.

> *I'm so angry that my body's all*
> *but bursting into flame.*
> —*Alamanda, French troubadour (1165-1199)*

About a decade ago, I spent the weekend with a friend on Long Island. Although Linda was younger than me, she was going through an early and apparently very difficult menopause that made her exhausted and physically uncomfortable most of the time. Her discomfort would have been enough to deal with, but her mother, with whom she shared an extremely troubled relationship, was in the process of dying. A professional nurse, Linda was taking care of her mother after work, while at the same time studying for her Ph.D. exams at night. The combination of these strains put her seriously over the edge, and she seethed from sunup to sundown. Though she did not take her anger out on me directly, I was surrounded and consumed by its intensity all the same. Ever since that painful weekend, I have been acutely aware of how many similarly furious women-of-a-certain-age I encounter as I go about my business. Not to mention the times when I surely could be counted among them.

The relentless bombardment of losses that batters us in every area of our lives effectively strips us of any unrealistic, immature confidence that we once might have had that we were safe in an unchanging and dependable world. Though we may have been shielded by our youthful sense of indestructibility as well as by our notoriously death-denying culture, we now understand, because we have experienced it, that nothing and no one stays the same forever, that all things must end sometime, that shit does, indeed, happen.

This rude lesson is brought home, more often than not, on the wings of death. When our parents sicken and die, they leave us standing alone and we cannot help but notice that we will be next to kick up our heels in the ancestral conga line. It is also common for us to start losing our husbands, friends, and contemporaries, which forces us with a mighty shove to confront our own fragile mortality. As even the relentlessly upbeat Doris Day noted, "The really frightening thing about middle age is the knowledge that you'll outgrow it."

Our watch sports a much larger face these days—not only because we have trouble seeing it, but because we are uncomfortably aware of time running out. In a flash, we realize that life has been moving along without us for quite some time now. We just weren't paying attention. We were busy, distracted by our responsibilities, lulled and dulled by our routines and addictions, deluded by denial. And, lo, before we realized what was happening, we had reached—no, probably bypassed—the halfway mark of our lives. From now on, we swear, we will make every precious second count.

The years seem to rush by now, and I think of death as a fast approaching end of a journey— double and treble reason for loving as well as working while it is day.

—George Eliot, English writer (1819-1880)

If we are unsure how to weather these crises, it is perhaps because so few women have had to face them before. The notion that fifty years of age could be considered a "halfway" mark is unprecedented. For most of human existence, life expectancy hovered at around twenty to thirty years, and it was only by 1800 that folks commonly began to live to be forty. American women now enjoy a mean life expectancy of eighty-four years, a stunning rise from only forty-eight years for a woman born in 1900. In general, women live about eight years longer than men, whose average life expectancy today is seventy-six years. It was once thought that when large numbers of women entered previously male-dominated professions, they, too, would start dropping dead of heart attacks and strokes on the stock exchange floor. Not only did that not happen, but women now outlive men by an even greater margin than before. Today, a woman is likely to live thirty-five to forty years following her menopause.

If a woman reaches fifty without a chronic illness, notes the well-known obstetrician-gynecologist, Dr. Christiane Northrup, in *The Wisdom of Menopause*, she has every expectation of living into her mid-eighties at least. Our chance these days of living to one hundred is one in fifty, an astronomical increase over the millennia from one in twenty million. This means that at midlife, we can typically expect two or three dynamic, active, productive decades before we consider ourselves old enough to claim the right to be called Crones. We do not look or feel or act our age because our age is no longer perceived to be old. Or, as the caption of a *New Yorker* cartoon put it, "Good news, honey—seventy is the new fifty." In Dr. Northrup's words, menopause is the "springtime of the second half of life."

But if we are blessed with this inestimable gift of many more years of life than anyone who ever lived on Earth before us could ever have imagined, it is crucial that we wend our way with great care through the crises of our midlife passage, so that we can learn how to turn our losses into the very lessons that will help us to achieve the life that we want for ourselves as we age. If we ignore our unresolved problems, chronic irritants, and burning resentments, we can be sure that they will surface as toxic stress that can cause cancer, heart attacks, substance abuse, depression, and other debilitating and life-threatening problems. How successfully we handle our changes now will determine the quality of our health and well-being for all of our future years. Our life literally depends on it.

Midlife women today are anxious to work through the potential panic of aging and its negative, derogatory cultural connotations with at least some measure of good grace. Possessing both the vital stamina of youth and the experienced wisdom of age, our pioneering generation is especially suited to such a task. Unique in history for our unprecedented freedom, education, individuality, worldliness, health, wealth, and longevity, we now hold positions of hard-earned authority, responsibility, and influence in ever-wider realms. Though certainly not perfect, nor perfectly safe, our power is unparalleled. Moreover, weaned on free thinking, idealism, and independence, we have been prescribing the parameters of our lives, inventing and reinventing our culture and ourselves for decades.

Now we are reaching maturity just in time to shape the new millennium for generations of women to come. And there are more of us every day. One third of all women in America are over the age of fifty, and one woman reaches that milestone every seven and a half seconds. As a matter of fact, climacteric women, sixty million strong, now comprise the single largest population segment of American society. Silent no more, we are reading and talking and conspiring among ourselves about how to best traverse this profound time in our lives. We want assurance that the difficult transitions we are experiencing might bring about a period of positive growth and transformation for ourselves as individuals, for our relationships, and for society as a whole. But how do we get there from here? Who can guide us? And where do we look for inspiration?

How helpful it would be to have a host of positive role models with whom we could identify as we strive to mold a satisfying and fulfilling middle and old age for ourselves and for future generations of women. Determined to redefine the parameters and archetypes of middle age, we will look to the past for grounding, to the future for courage, to each other for inspiration, and to ourselves for the answers.

One day, you finally knew what you had to do, and began.

—Mary Oliver, American poet (1935-)

CHAPTER 2

Reverence to Her

MYTHOLOGY, THE MATRIARCHY, AND ME

Woman is the creator of the universe,
the universe is her form;
woman is the foundation of the world,
she is the true form of the body.

—Saktisangama Tantra
Traditional Hindu scripture

S earch as we might, it is practically impossible to find historical examples of vigorous and influential women in their middle years, and unfortunately, the body of common folklore is equally bereft of potent female prototypes that might inspire us to follow in their paths. But where history fails us in our pursuit of appropriate role models for our new middle age, herstory offers us a mighty example of female power and primacy.

Contemporary women are drawn in ever-increasing numbers to the archetype of humanity's first divinity, the ancient Great Goddess in Her many guises. She offers us the ideal that we so desperately seek of female strength and wisdom, inspiration, and empowerment that can guide us through life's harrowing changes. Coming from a society, as we do, that often ignores, denies, and belittles our status as women, simply being conscious of another time when the female principle was revered as sacred and all-powerful is heartening. When we connect to the time of Goddess worship, suggests Merlin Stone in her seminal book, *When God Was a Woman*, we can access a rock-solid base of spiritual sustenance and emotional support with which we can identify and upon which we might model our lives.

In the beginning, people prayed to the Creatress of Life, the Mistress of Heaven. At the very dawn of religion, God was a woman. Do you remember?
—*Merlin Stone, British-American writer (Twentieth Century)*

IN THE BEGINNING

Once upon a time, as the legends of peoples around the globe attest, in the very dawn of human time and culture, there was a Great Mother who gave birth to the Earth and all who dwell upon it. She bore the skies, the heavenly realms, and the celestial bodies that endlessly circle in space. The Divine Creative Power of the universe was surely, clearly, indubitably female and honored by women and men alike throughout the millennia. It is the female of every species, after all—human included—who is capable of producing young. We are somehow able to fashion from ourselves the stuff of life, to bear from our own blood and body an entirely new generation. And as if that weren't amazing enough, we manage to manufacture and dispense an abundant supply of the very substance of sustenance, allowing us to continue to nurture our consummate creations. Above all, the female is prolific, capable of repeating this entire miraculous process again and again.

Is this not the way of Nature Herself? Does She not constantly produce and provide? Reproduce and recycle? Engender and embrace? The Earth is alive with the inconceivable multitudes of animals, vegetables, and minerals, the skies teeming with Her brilliant creations. Nature, then, *must* be female. Mother Nature, Mother Earth, is celebrated by many cultures as the prime creatrix, the giver of all life. The Greek historian Herodotus wrote that all of the known names for the Earth were female, while Homer uttered Her praises, "I shall sing of Gaia, Universal Mother, firmly founded, Oldest of all the Holy Ones." The African Ashanti call Her Asase Ya. "We got everything from Asase Ya," they say, "food, water: we rest upon Her when we die."

Wide-ranging creation myths describe how the Earth was made from Her sacred body. According to the Apaches, all creatures came from the Earth, "just like a child being born from its mother." Asintmah, the first woman of the Athapascan peoples of Western Canada and Alaska, was midwife to Mother Earth. During Her confinement, Asintmah wove for Her a great blanket and laid it carefully across the body of the Earth Mother. She then reached under this birthing blanket and pulled out a mouse, followed by a rabbit, and then, one by one, She brought forth each of the Earth's vast multitude from the loins of the Great Mother. It is said of Mother Earth that She created all there is and Her Great Spirit inhabits all that She created.

Mother's milk, as the primordial generative substance, is the theme of creation myths throughout Europe, Africa, the Middle East, Egypt, Greece, India, and Japan. "I am your mother, I fed you in times of famine, now I go back to my land," sings the Milk Bird in the Lesotho legend from southern Africa. Stories from both Iran and Siberia describe a sacred celestial Milk Lake from which all life emerged and is eternally nourished. Sweet fresh water that formed the streams, lakes, and rivers issued forth from the swollen breasts of Yemonja, Mother of Earth, according to the Ifa religion of the Yuruba peoples of Nigeria. The Babylonians pictured the Mother Goddess with breasts so big with milk that She had to support them with both hands.

Humankind, in its infancy, clung to the primal comprehension of a maternal Earth, in the same way that any completely dependent child hangs onto her mother's hip. Faced with the reality of the harshness of life and our utter reliance upon the whims and vagaries of the natural forces around us, we held on for dear life. This archetype has been celebrated for so long, and is still so resonant to so many, because it holds some deeply essential, primal validity. It offers the truths and well-worn wisdom that speak to us on the most profound level. This, of course, is the very definition of an archetype.

Read and hear assiduously the divine lessons...
to gather from them precious daisies for your ears
and make from them rings and bracelets.
—*Caesarea, French Abbess of St. Jean of Arles*
(c. Sixth Century)

In the fourth century BC, the Greek philosopher Plato was the first to identify the idea of archetypes, or, as he called them, Forms. He defined a Form as an eternal description of an abstract concept such as Beauty, that remains unchanging despite the variety of permutations that might manifest in its name. The twentieth-century psychologist Carl Jung developed a more complex system of archetypes, which he derived from the universal roles played by people at different times in life, such as the Mother, the Child, the Trickster, the Servant, the Warrior, the Sage. In addition to our own unique unconscious selves, he wrote, "There exists a second psychic system of a collective, universal, and impersonal nature that is identical in all individuals." In these archetypes, we recognize parts of ourselves. Ultimately, archetypes ring true, because they are now and always have been true.

The archetypal Great Mother, creatrix of all existence, matriarch of the races of goddesses and gods, spirits and weather, humans and other animals, reigned supreme everywhere until the patriarchal revolution, only about five thousand years ago, when She was replaced by a global pantheon of male godheads. Ancient depictions of Her, some 30,000 to 50,000 years old, worked in stone and bone and rendered in pigment on the walls of caves and rock outcroppings, are abundant throughout Africa, Old Europe, and Asia. These icons of humankind's first Supreme Being are extremely diverse, but She was universally regarded with reverence and deference as a living model mother.

Although She was commonly seen as the primary source, the original life force, She was never portrayed as being singular. Her power rests not in Her individuality, but in Her universality. The ultimate shape-shifter, Her persona was permeable. Numerous early depictions of Her were generic, completely faceless, but with the form and attitude of Her body clearly conveying Her attributes. Those representations that did possess facial features were each unique, with no two alike in the particulars. The ancient Goddess wore the face of woman—any woman, all women, Every Woman —expressing the sacred powers of the female forces in the Universe and reflecting the highest potential inherent in the lives of ordinary women.

You are the heaven and You are the earth,
You are the day and You are the night,
You are all pervading air,
You are the sacred offering of rice and flowers
  and of water;
You are Yourself all in all,
What can I offer You?
—Lalla Ded, Kashmiri yogini
  (Fourteenth Century)

The All-in-One Goddess

Mother Earth, Mother Nature, the Great Creation Goddess, is erratic in Her disposition as well as in Her persona, Her moods fluctuating as those of any woman might. Her emotions, like the weather, are mutable and span the full spectrum. She rainbow-glows, radiant in health and beauty. She twinkles like the stars, sparkles with good grace and joy. She is full and abundant, warm of spirit, and kind. She grows overcast, gets dark, oblique, breezy, and cool. She weeps with dew. She simmers and hisses on slow burn. She vents Her steam. She quakes in anger. She rumbles and grumbles and tears the house down. She sparks, bursts, erupts, explodes, implodes in passion. She can be gentle, generous, humorous, dependable, destructive and very, very scary. Sound like anyone we know?

Unlike the more rigidly defined male deities who followed Her in time, the Goddess has always been viewed as changeable, variable, and ever-evolving, constant—like life itself—only in Her change. Her shifts in personality, countenance, and mood are metaphoric reflections of the cyclic transformation and continual renewal evident in the natural world. She was widely associated with the constantly shifting visage of the moon and also with the changeable seas that rise up to meet it, those never-still waters flowing back and forth under the powerful lunar influence. As Moon Goddess, She has been known variously as Luna, Europa, Ariadne, Diana, Ishtar, Isis, Artemis, and a hundred other names. As Goddess of the Flowing Waters and the Generative Seas, She was Anuket, the Egyptian Goddess of the Fertile Nile. In Japan, She was the Ocean Goddess Benten, and in Babylon, She was Tiamat, Goddess of the Salty Seas who gave birth to the world.

In Babylon, Egypt, Libya, India, Greece, Lithuania, China, Mexico, and in many parts of Africa, She was portrayed as a Snake who sheds its skin and thus represents the power of transformation. In Egyptian hieroglyphics, the symbol of a cobra stands for "goddess." She was shown in such divergent cultures as Minoan, Cypriat, Cretan, Czechoslovakian, Aztec, Greek, Hopi, and Irish as a butterfly who is able to metamorphose in shape, form, and function. In *The Goddesses and Gods of Old Europe*, the noted archeologist Marija Gimbutas writes that the butterfly "image of the goddess has an early philosophical connection between cyclic lunar time and the regenerative role of the goddess in cycles of birth, death, and rebirth." As such, She was the obvious personification of the archetype of Change itself.

Changing Woman, or Estsanatlehi (Self-Renewing One) as She is called by the native peoples of the Southwest, is a Goddess for All Seasons. She represents the eternal great round, the whole and all of its constituent parts. She stands for the spinning cyclic ways of Nature. As Painted Woman, White Shell Woman, and Turquoise Woman, She represents the ever-evolving colors of the seasons of the year as She changes Her dress. Her symbols include the spiral that swirls as She does, the moon that mutates as She does, and the snake that sheds its skin and renews itself repeatedly as does She. It is said of Her, "She changes everything She touches, and everything She touches, changes."

A Goddess is great, indeed, who can change with the winds, with the times, with the tides, with the moon. Who can evolve and respond to meet the requirements and needs of any situation, any population, and every station of life. The examples and lessons of Her cyclic expression are utterly true. Life *does* equal change. As we cycle through life, we all grow to know that nothing ever stays the same, including ourselves. The archaic Great Goddess in Her many manifestations has long reflected and reinforced our own physical, mental, emotional, and spiritual changeability, as well as the external transformations in the world around us. This knowledge and acceptance of change is the greatest gift of the Great Goddess.

The all-encompassing spirit of the original Great Goddess of All Creation eventually diversified and specialized, evolving into an extended sisterhood of complex, multi-dimensional, conglomerate goddesses, each with intricate suites of identity, personality, preference, and power. She is the One Who is Many, the Many Who are One. She has a thousand appellations, and for each name, she has a special interest, a totem animal, a favorite flower or tree or fruit, and is associated with a particular day of the week, season of the year, phase of the moon, or cycle of life. The Goddess of Life, Death, and Infinity became the Goddesses of Love, Sex, Birth, Agriculture, Fishing, Weaving, Fortune, Fate, Fury, and other aspects. Each of Her dimensions is a fully formed archetype of its own, individual and unique, yet indivisible, related to every other aspect and to the shared source of female power.

Among the pantheon of female deities there are a multitude of goddesses who specifically represent the different stages and circumstances of the life cycle of women. In each of Her many aspects, She bestows a divine wisdom to the women who turn to Her, to those who feel aligned and identified with Her province. For ages, this archetypal goddess has offered women guidance and support at every turn as we progress along the pathways of our lives. Reflecting upon Her images and stories, we can see the continuum of our own development. She stands for us at each pivotal point in our journey and stands with us in validation of our personal needs along the way. In Her stages we see the cycles of time and space and all reality. Moreover, She keeps us connected, as an archetype does, to the essential center of our being, the very meaning of our lives.

A Creed for Free Women
(*and such men as feel happy with it)

I am.
I am from and of The Mother.
I am as I am.
Wilfully harming none, none may question me.
As no free-growing tree serves another or requires to be served.
As no lion or lamb or mouse is bound or binds,
No plant or blade of grass nor ocean fish,
So I am not here to serve or be served.

I am Child of every Mother,
Mother of each daughter,
Sister of every woman,
And lover of whom I choose or chooses me.
She we have called Goddess for human comprehension.
We do the work of The Mother,
Together or alone we dance Her Dance,
She, the Source, never-to-be-grasped Mystery,
Terrible Cauldron, Womb,
Spinning out of her the unimaginably small
And the immeasurably vast—
Galaxies, worlds, flaming suns—
And our Earth, fertile with her beneficence,
Here, offering tenderest flowers.
(Yet flowers whose roots may split rock.)
I, we, Mothers, Sisters, Lovers,
Infinitely small out of her vastness,
Yet our roots too may split rock,
Rock of the rigid, the oppressive
In human affairs.
Thus is She
And being of Her
Thus am I.
Powered by Her,
As she gives, I may give,
Even of my blood and breath:
But none may require it;
And none may question me.
I am.
I am That I am.

   —Elsa Gidlow, American poet (1898–1986)

THE TRIPLE GODDESS

Though many aspects of the Goddess are specific to a particular time and place, climate and culture, those personas that mirror the stages of a woman's life are particularly widespread. Three of the most pervasive aspects, repeated countless times in myths from around the world, are those of the young girl or Maiden (often referred to as the Virgin), the pregnant or nursing Mother, and the wizened hag or the Crone. In some instances, these are identified as the three faces of a single powerful female deity. Three is a power number, representing as it does the All as opposed to the One or the Both. There is a sense of completeness inherent in three. According to mathematical theory, a single occurrence is of no statistical significance, a second occurrence might be merely a coincidence, but a third occurrence suggests an immutable law.

It was common in many cultures to view deities as triads, but they did not necessarily characterize different ages and stations of life. Rather, they most frequently represented some sort of alliance or familial relationship. Many of the Roman Trios were more like sororities of associates than differentiated age models. The Three Sirens are depicted as a bevy of beauties all around the same age, as are the Three Graces, known as Aglaia (Splendor), Euphrosyne (Mirth), and Thalia (Good Cheer), who all represent similar light-hearted dispositions. The Three Furies, or the Erinnyes, were fearsome, snake-haired, winged avengers known as Alecto (the Resentful), Megaera (the Relentless), and Tisiphone (the Revenger).

One version of the Roman Triple Goddess persists in Western civilization as the well-known Three Fates. Though paintings of the Three Fates on vases and friezes show all three women as lovely nymphs, the familiar myth actually describes the trio as: the young and slender Lacheses, who rules all things past, spinner of the thread of life; the ripe Clotho, the overseer of all things present, who holds the spool and measures the thread; and the withered Atropos, sovereign of things to come, who snips the thread, severing the cord of life.

She Who is Maiden, Mother, and Crone is associated with Celtic, Greek, Roman, and Indian traditions. The Hindu/Buddhist three-headed Kali is the oldest of the Triple Goddesses. She is sometimes seen as Parvati the Creator, attended by nubile young priestesses or yoginis. She is Durga the Preserver, served by the Matri, the Mothers. And she is Uma the Destroyer honored by the Dakinis, or elder Skywalkers. To the Irish, She is the triple Morrigan, a notorious shape-shifting warrior goddess whose name means "Great Queen." Her three parts include Anu or Danu, the wild Maiden, Babd, the fertile, fiercely protective Mother, and Macha, the Crone destroyer, grim reaper of the dead.

Today, this triple Maiden-Mother-Crone model is at the root of the Goddess-identified spirituality movement worldwide. The beliefs and practices of the many adherents, women and men alike, of Wiccan, Pagan, and other popular Earth Religions are permeated with the tri-level Goddess paradigm. Seen as the original Holy Trinity, She is—in turn and at once—the young Maiden, representing development, expansion, and all things new; the fertile Mother, standing for creation, procreation, maintenance, and nourishment; and the old Crone, wise in the ways of the world, who dies to be reborn in future generations. The three together reflect a completeness of life that is a powerful source of sustenance, understanding, acceptance, respect, and support for women who see in Her cycles reflections of our own.

The young girl, the Maiden, is the dawn, fresh with dew, alive with surprise. She is innocent, a virgin, a sweet bird of youth. She is the model of formation and growth, aspiration and new beginnings, innocence and exploration. Like the Greek Persephone and Artemis, She is Goddess of spring and the waxing moon, inducted at Her first blood. As Flora and Diana in Rome and Chimalman and Xochiquetzal in Aztec Mexico, She represents the potential, the inherent possibilities in life, the bud, the shoot, the egg, the energy, the ultimate hope. She is forever young, keeper of the

Tree of Life with its apples of immortality. Untouched, born of blossoms, Her smooth perfection unmarred, She serves as the maid of initiation ceremonies in many cultures.

Free-spirited and unselfconscious, the Maiden pursues Her own interests and pleasures without permission and without guilt. She discovers and exploits the seductive power of Her newly discovered sexuality and She does it brazenly, and on Her own terms. Her vitality, enthusiasm and willingness to explore and experiment are among Her finest charms. There is an aura of enchantment about Her, and unbridled excitement. Like the tennis stars Venus and Serena Williams, today's Maiden daughters are bold, unabashed, and unashamed, flexing the muscles of their considerable incipient power.

The Mother, the Matron, whose ranks include the well-known Egyptian Isis, who gave birth to the sun, Her son, as well as the Greek Demeter, Hestia, and Hera, and the Roman Juno and Vesta, typifies fertility, abundance, sexuality, maternity, manifestation, nurturing, and domesticity. Goddess of the full moon, of summer, She is in full flower, lush with the stuff, the sweet nectar of life. The Good Mother not only produces life, She nourishes it, provides for it, cares for it, monitors its growth. And, like the Hindu Warrior Goddess Durga who rides a tiger into battle to defend Her children, She secures their safety and well-being fearlessly and, if necessary, against all odds. She is the grand creator, the limitlessly fecund archetype of the fertile aspects of Nature. Mothering puts us in a state of supreme response-ability, where our fierce love, dependability, and solidity produces, projects, and protects a positive impact on our immediate charge, be it a community, a career, or a child.

Traditionally initiated with the menopausal loss of Her blood, the Crone is the old one, wise with age, astute with experience, unrelenting with the knowledge of reality. She personifies the dark lessons of destruction, death, and decay, and prepares the way for an ultimate regeneration. She reminds us that what is given is also taken, and She takes as much as

She gives. Her job is to guide the dead, to escort them on their way back into Her body, which is the barren cold Earth in winter. In Libya, She was recognized as Ament the Hawk Goddess who sat in a tree at the edge of the desert, where She welcomed the newly deceased at the gates of the underworld. In the frozen Arctic, She is Sedna who sits at the bottom of the sea accompanied by Her seals, who will stir up great storms and suck hunters down to Her depths if She is not placated. She is the Japanese Fuji and the Hawaiian Pele who rage and blow deadly steam and lava. She is often the frightful, hateful hag of destruction.

Like the dying dark moon, She closes in on Herself in order to be able to digest and distribute what She has learned in Her many years, Her many tears. She is the model of reflection, introspection, evaluation, retrenchment, and repose. She Who Remembers is the collector and dispenser of all accumulated knowledge. Her wisdom of the workings of the wheels of time, season, and cycle, make Her kind in the end, and compassionate. She has seen it all and understands, empathizes, commiserates. We see our aging form in Her and are inspired to accept the changes in the world and in ourselves. She whispers to us the scary truths that we wish to ignore, and we listen, for Hers is the voice of the wisdom of the ages: "All times must pass and all things must die."

Help us to be ever faithful gardeners of the spirit, who know that without darkness nothing comes to birth, and without light nothing flowers.
—*May Sarton, American writer (1902-1995)*

Who Is the Triple Goddess to Us?

For millennia, these three faces of the original Goddess have accurately reflected the stages of women's lives—the developing youth, the nurturing mother, and the wise old woman. Most celebrants in the various female spirituality, Earth-based, pagan, and witchcraft-of-all-stripes communities have adopted the Triple Goddess as their own. To this formative batter, they have added several parts of Celtic, Greek, Egyptian, and Hindu mythology and baked themselves a three-layer Goddess Cake to feast on. This rich concoction has been gobbled up with such gusto because it has been the only widely served confection of a powerful female divinity, which women crave as much as chocolate. She has fed and nurtured the spiritually hungry, and for this marvelous sustenance, She is much beloved.

Even today, She corresponds with the real life expectancy and experience of most women in the world who live pretty much as they always have. The reality of their existence dictates that they grow quickly through girlhood into early and prolonged maternity, then, if they are lucky enough to survive multiple childbirths and general poverty, they pass through menopause directly into old age. As recently as the early 1900s, the average age of menopause was forty-six and the life expectancy for women was only fifty-one. Photographs of my own grandmother, when she was younger than I am now, picture a matronly-looking lady with the Old Worldly, stately countenance of a grandmother, a bubby, an abuela— a full decade before I was born. Part of her elderly appearance is purely the style of the period, the rest a reflection of her hard life and times.

But as popular as She has proven Herself to be, however much Her devotees are moved to protect and preserve Her image, it seems to me that the Triple Goddess has perhaps outlived Her relevance to many of us in the modern world. Now that women of my generation are reaching our menopause, we have quite a few questions about the validity of the Three Stage Goddess for our lives, considering that an entire major stage—*our* stage—is missing from the construct. We haven't been Maidens for decades, and we are no longer Mother material either. Nor are we anywhere near being old. Sure, some creative minds have tried to bridge the gap—I recently read an article in a women's spirituality journal entitled "The Three Seasons of a Woman's Life: Spring, Summer, and Fallwinter"— but identifying ourselves as Baby Crones, Juicy Crones, Spice Crones, or Crones of any other stripe, simply sidesteps the issue.

While certainly there is still much to learn from the Maiden-Mother-Crone model, the old triple-header construct is no longer all-inclusive. It doesn't describe my life or the lives of other contemporary women in their middle years living in modern industrialized countries. It does not address our issues and needs, nor does it embrace our unique and unprecedented dynamic position in society. It does not even recognize our existence.

Even women for whom the Triple Goddess has been, until now, a perfect metaphoric guide are beginning to realize that we have outgrown Her restrictive dimensions. Her three-sided nature limits us just when we are throwing off the yokes of all predictability. Recently, a reader of the journal *SageWoman* highlighted our dilemma. "I have never felt comfortable with the Crone," she wrote. "Now that I am in my fifties I finally understand why…. I hope someday to be a Crone when I'm in my eighties or nineties. For now, my life is filled with creative activity, new undertakings, career change, and still to be explored freedoms. Long before I enter the age of Crone I hope to be healer and teacher, to kick up my heels in the dance of the wild woman and savor new adventures 'Running Wild with the Wolves.'"

We are a huge population of incredibly mighty women coming into the fullest power of our prime. "One's prime is elusive," warns the colorful headmistress in Muriel Spark's *The Prime of Miss Jean Brody*. "You little girls when you grow up, you must be on the alert to recognize your prime at whatever time of your life it may occur. You must then live it to the full."

Most of us modern midlife women have never looked or felt better, nor have we been nearly so effective.

Clearly it is time for a paradigm shift. Life is about nothing if not change, which is the greatest teaching of the cyclical Goddess, after all. Her power and inspiration are found in Her infinite flexibility, Her adept adaptability, Her unbounded ability to always change. As Shirley MacLaine once commented, "Someday perhaps change will occur when times are ready for it instead of always when it is too late. Someday change will be accepted as life itself." The Great Goddess, supreme mistress of the art of transformation, will surely respond to the changes in our lives and times by enlarging the vision of Herself to embody Her own fourth dimension, and ours. The Great Goddess is, even now, beginning to expand to include us in Her archetypal embrace.

Life is an enfoldment, and the further we travel the more truth we comprehend. To understand the things that are at our door is the best preparation for understanding those things that lie beyond.

—*Hypatia, Egyptian philosopher and scientist (370-417)*

CHAPTER 3

Enter the Queen

CREATING A MODERN MYTHIC MODEL

*A great wind is blowing, and that gives
you either imagination or a headache.*
—*Catherine the Great, Empress of Russia (1729-1796)*

Exempted from once-upon-a-time ideas about aging due to our vast-ly expanded life expectancy, contemporary women in our middle years find ourselves afloat, drifting somewhere between life stages with no archetypal raft to grab onto. No longer sprite Maidens, nor fertile Mothers, we enter our middle years with great trepidation, given that the popular media has typically portrayed menopausal women as over-the-hill, over-wrought—flakes or furies—completely undesirable in either case. But, then, what are we if we are not Crones?

Myths, tales, and historical records featuring positive depictions of powerful middle-aged female figures are few and far between. There is no herstory relating a sisterhood of midlife goddesses, no codified body of lit-erature to which we can turn for affirmative examples of a profound and potent midlife. Real life role models are sparse, as well, although there cer-tainly have always been, in every era and society, remarkable exceptions—powerful middle-aged women who were rulers, adventurers, artists, entre-preneurs, scientists, spiritual leaders—mature, glamorous, and courageous sheroes of all stripes.

The extended and vigorous midlife period that we are now beginning to experience is largely unaccounted for in myth and archetype for the simple reason that such longevity has never before occurred for great masses of women as a whole. Poised on the brink of uncharted waters, we desperately need a new body of role models, examples, and teachers to encourage us as we explore the unfamiliar landscape of our changing lives and begin to create new and joyful ways of being in charge of our own destinies. Bereft of affirming depictions of our lives, today's women of a certain age are more than ready, willing, and perfectly capable of creating our own.

If there's a book you really want to read, but it hasn't been written yet, then you must write it.
—*Toni Morrison, American writer (1931-)*

THE DAWN OF AWARENESS

It was through my own process of coming of age that I began to question the Triple Goddess archetype. My own Maiden and Motherhood periods, while perhaps individualistic, were true to the universal archetypes that define them, but they led me down a path that hardly left me feeling at midlife like the wise and wizened Crone.

My Maiden years were devoted largely to my developing curiosity about the world around me, the greater universe and its workings, and especially my perfect place in it all. Introspective and intuitive ever since I was very young, I received little understanding or support for my strong spiritual nature from my own family or the middle class Cleveland community where we lived. On the surface, life in my dysfunctional two-parent family, which then became a single-working-mother-with-two-kids-household, was normal, average, and typically suburban, but like other children under similar circumstances, I constructed my own secret internal world of fantasy and wonder. Left to my own soul survival devices, I kept journals of my thoughts and dreams and composed poems and affirmations to give myself courage and hope. I built private backyard sanctuaries and created quirky altars in basements, in attics, and then in my dorm rooms at Ohio State University, where, to the horror of my smirking roommates, I lit candles, meditated, and performed my home-grown ceremonies.

As soon as I left home for college, my life became my own and I was determined to live it on my own terms. Though I had been an instinctive spiritual seeker for most of my life, I had never been free enough to dedicate myself so completely, so conscientiously, so passionately to the practice of self-knowledge and actualization. I was a young woman on a sacred quest to find my authentic Self and to begin to live the life that I was meant to live. Whatever, wherever, however that might be. Once I got going, I was on a roll. I challenged myself to expand all of my horizons and indulged myself in endlessly fascinating explorations of inner and outer space, conducted on physical, intellectual, emotional, psychic, sexual, and geographic terrain.

My focus was not entirely internal. Like many other women of my free-love generation, I experimented widely, wildly, with sex. But by the age of thirty, I had left an idiotic mistake of a marriage and several semi-serious boyfriends behind. Like Greta Garbo, I "vanted to be alone." Those relationships were not awful or abusive or co-dependent or any such thing. They just didn't fulfill me, the full me. Something crucial was always missing. Eventually, I began to realize that the absent ingredient was me. How I yearned to return to myself, in the true heart of my soul and not as a warped reflection of someone else's view of me, be it a mother's or a lover's or *Glamour* magazine's. In an undeniable flash of inner truth and commanding clarity, I felt myself called upon by spirit, by destiny, by dharma, by fate, by free will, to embark upon a concerted search and rescue mission for the

Holy Grail of my own elusive soul. And this expedition had to be solo.

As I prayed to the universe to "show me the way," I traveled on pig and chicken buses to holy sites on far continents. In jungles and deserts I sought out teachers of the old ways, like my Mazatec shaman mentor, Maria Sabina, and I found inspiration in the beloved figure of the Virgin of Guadalupe. I retreated to mud and wattle huts on the tops of mountains. I performed intricate acts of private devotion and endurance: silent retreats, long fasts, arduous vigils, vision quests, pilgrimages. Like the Greek Maiden Moon Goddess Artemis, the Virgin Huntress, I was a free and wild spirit running through the mysterious night forest, beholden to none and learning how to be sufficient unto myself. "Feed me," I whispered, and I did. I surrounded myself with banquets of inspiration and enrichment, beauty, philosophy, music, and science. By doing t'ai chi and yoga, I strengthened my body and became more flexible and balanced. Studying comparative religion, multi-cultural myth and ritual, anthropology, astronomy, and quantum physics did the same for my brain.

What I did for myself, I did for others as well. Eventually, rich with adventure and experience and motivated by the archetypal call of the Mother's need to nest, I returned home to Exotic Brooklyn to establish a more sedentary, domestic life for myself. I engaged in life-affirming activities: made art and ceremony, built a home, a makeshift family, a community, and a professional ritual practice.

I was thirty-five years old and in love, but in a new way. I knew who I was and was secure in that Self-knowledge. This time around, I felt safe enough in my own embrace to open my heart and lower my defenses and let my lover into my life with no fear of losing my own center, establishing a couplehood that is still alive and well to this day, despite, or more likely because of, the fact that we chose not to live together. More secure in my increasingly mature Self and my relationship, I extended my affection and protection to a number of children and young people whose presence enlivened my heart and home. A much-loved foster son moved in with me at ten and stayed until he went away to school at sixteen, and I mentored other high school and college interns and assistants at what I came to call the Auntie Mame Mama Donna School of Life.

At the same time, I established a ritual consultancy, ceremonial center, and healing haven, a safe space where others could come to celebrate the cycles of the cosmos according to the world's beliefs and satisfy their own spiritual longings. In the intimacy of my ceremonial center and in the public parks and plazas of New York City, I sought to share traditional wisdom passed down from ancient cultures through the ages, with a very modern, very stressed out, but very hungry urban community. With the strength acquired from these many nourishing connections, I gradually came to claim and honor my Mother power. Daughter of Mother Earth Herself, I lavished love and sex and healing on everyone around me.

But by the time I was forty, my golden days of Motherhood had dimmed. Death came into my life as family members, friends, and students fell ill all around me. For the next decade and a half, my main focus and concentration went toward easing the way of death. Mama Donna to my extended clan, I held the hands and rubbed the feet of the sick and the scared. I read, talked, and chanted to the dying and sat with them in silence. I laid out the bodies, counseled the grief-stricken, wrote obituaries, and officiated at funerals and memorials. By the time I reached my fifties, I was still a bleeding woman, though mostly hemorrhaging from my heart.

I had just spent a fifteen-year eternity on the deathwatch, losing nearly everyone and everything that I loved and I was struggling to climb up from the dismal abyss of my multi-layered grief. I had lost my family, friends, pets, my homemade home of eighteen years, my communal community, my emotional support system of spirit sisters, many of my precarious sources of income, my monthly blood, my hormones, my equilibrium, my figure, my youth, my confidence, and whatever control I thought I had exerted over my life.

It is hard enough as a spiritual counselor to minister to pain, fear, and grief with a clear head and steady nerves, but I was a walking wreck. My interminable insomnia, insufferable mood swings, and hormonal surprise attacks definitely did not help. All of my energy was lavished on others, who were, it seemed, literally dying to leave me. My own needs were relinquished, forgotten, forgone. Sometime during that interminable period, somewhere along the way between making Jell-O, changing invalid diapers, and scattering ashes, I lost my center, I am sorry to say, and some of my hard-won Self as well. I was off kilter and shaky, preoccupied with the process of disease, decline, death, and decay—my own included. I had forgotten all about life and living.

To top it off, I was all but celibate for long patches of time, totally disinclined to engage sexually. Although surely sex could have been a salve in such hard times, I refused the comforts that were offered, and retreated like a turtle into the shell of my sad self. Rarely in the mood, I was too tired, too busy, too upset and distracted. And the people in my most intimate life, friends and lover alike—those who were still standing—fled from me, I noticed regretfully, frightened by my hands-on association with so much pain and suffering, as if death were a contagious disease. All I managed to attract was trouble.

When a big thing falls it falls big, big,
and it rains, it rains. and it's not beaten,
and the earth just keeps curling around itself...
—Simone Forti, American dancer and
movement theorist (1935-)

Caught in the wasteland, the endless morass at the bottom of that dark pit of terror, I gradually became completely paralyzed, unable to help myself, too heartbroken even to lick my own wounds. One by one, just when I needed them the most, I let go of everything that I had learned to depend on to soothe, support, and uplift myself in times of trouble. In addition to sex, I gave up yoga, t'ai chi, swimming, workouts, vitamins, movies, walking in nature, and even taking my favorite hour-long baths. Resentment and bitterness began to tinge the edges of my anguish. "Self-pity in its early stages is as snug as a feather mattress," warns Maya Angelou. "Only when it hardens does it become uncomfortable." The result of this self-destructive foolhardiness was an inevitable downward spiral into despair.

In the end, I was no Mother Teresa. My anger roiled to the surface, which served only to attract negative vibes and random volatility from total strangers. Once while I was shopping, a crotchety old woman actually started screaming at me, flailing at me with her handbag for no earthly reason except that "I was asking for it," as if she could see the dark clouds swirling through my mind. I hadn't said a word to her, but I was prickly as hell and she felt it. It takes one to know one. And I knew myself to be at the ugly end of my desperate rope.

An ox at the roadside, when it is dying of hunger and thirst, does not lie down; it walks up and down, up and down, seeking—it knows not what—but it does not lie down.
—Olive Schreiner, South African novelist and feminist (1855-1920)

THE QUEEN REVEALED

Then, one day, I'd had enough. "Okay, Donna," I scolded myself. "Let's get a grip. Enough is enough, already." I was finally and completely disgusted with my sorryass self. "Yes, some terrible things have happened. Okay, *lots* of terrible things happened. Life happened. Why should I be exempt? Get over it and move on already. After all, I am still here, alive. It is everyone else who is dead." While true in many ways, my impatient response mainly revealed my desire to be free of the pain. But you can't just brush grief away and deny it access to your heart. You have to allow yourself to open fully to it, to feel it, really feel it with each fiber of your being, to be down in there rolling around in the mud with it, in order to benefit from the many lessons that loss has to teach.

Resolute, I began my struggle to repossess all of the body-mind-heart-spirit support skills that I had so recklessly tossed aside during my tortured middle years. I craved quiet time out and serious sustenance to help me process all that I had seen, been, done, and felt. I needed to just be still and see what I could see. I call this discipline Sitting in the Shadows.

Grieving is an active practice, a conscious engagement that comes from a place of tenderness, compassion, and love, and not the same thing at all as wallowing in formless self-pity, bitterness, and anger. As I grieved, I began to open to my pain and I started to understand that to acknowledge our grief and our pain, our fears and our foibles, our vulnerability and our utter weakness, is ultimately our greatest strength and certainly our best hope for maturation, expansion, and wisdom.

Time's violence rends the soul;
through the rent eternity enters.
—Simone Weil, French philosopher (1909-1943)

I drew in on myself, determined to process my thoughts and emotions. Out came my neglected journal and I embraced it as a long-lost, much-missed friend. I sought council between its covers and absorbed myself in its pages, seeking to find the way back to my misaligned center, my sanity, and my true Self. I examined the recent events in my life, as well as my response and reactions to them. Yes, it is true, I had been called to the task. Yes, I did rise to meet each occasion. Yes, I had even succeeded in being of some considerable support. I also acknowledged my experience and affirmed my feelings of being completely helpless. I had been to hell and back—alone. All the support that I had ever known in my life was going, going, gone. Which, of course, in retrospect, was precisely the lesson that I was meant to learn—to be able to rely on myself alone.

In looking back with honesty, I realized that I had been extraordinarily lucky, blessed by loving, caring friends and a supportive community. There had always been, my entire adult life, someone to turn to, and it was no wonder that I was bereft when that was no longer the case. But at the end of the day, I had to learn how to stand on my own two feet and face what I might. This terrible transition was a proficiency test in the school of life. Unless we are challenged, how else can we ever realize our capabilities? Why would we bother? Gradually, over time, I grew to embrace the difficult circumstances that had been forced upon me, as well as the hard changes wrought from within, for the invaluable opportunities for growth and spiritual development that they offered.

By day I did what I had to in the hospice zone and at night I tried to write. Like Penelope, I spent my evenings alone in the dark, spinning yarns, weaving a comforting sense of order, pattern, and systematic interconnectivity around myself like a shawl, a silk cocoon. I sat in its embrace, quietly quilting my own experience into the intricate complexity, the enduring continuity of That Which Is, looking for meaning, direction, and perception. Like Madame Lafarge, I was knitting a running commentary on the revolution of my life, my duel with death, as a way to interpret the rules of engagement and the lessons of the fray. By handling the threads and passing the shuttle, I was attempting to re-weave what had been broken, and to repair the damage that I had both incurred and inflicted as a result of my pain.

Penelope in her dreams unweaves
What her suitors bid her weave each day,
But no longer waits for Ulysses,
Taking the long way home.
She is making her own life,
Building a kiln for her voyage
Shaping herself on the potter's wheel,
Adding daily more clay from the earth.
Her first joy is to create herself.
If Ulysses returns, she will be his equal.
He who has braved the sea & she the fire
Will have ways of knowing each other.

—Karen Ethelsdattar, American poet (1954-)

The era of my selfless mothering of others was coming to an end and I began more and more to direct my ministering attentions toward my own bruised and battered Self. I had been a good mother, a good daughter, a good friend, a good partner and lover, a good girl all around, for so long, so, so very long. I had dedicated my life to the healing, the needing, of others—usually to the exclusion of my own self-regard. And my own abused, overworked body and poor broken heart were crying out for mending, for compassionate convalescence. Now that I was motherless, it was time to claim the responsibility for my own care and feeding, my own growth and comfort, my own self-healing.

Though not unscathed, I had endured the onslaught of my terrible trials by fire and survived my middle passage of the soul. Slowly I learned—and am still learning—how to mother myself, to lavish upon myself that same unconditional loving kindness, encouragement, support, and solace that I have always given so freely to others. I began to feel good about what

I had achieved. I felt that I could do anything, because, in fact, I had. Gradually, after all that anguish, I began to find my easy stride again and was trotting along with new authority, enjoyment, and aplomb. Ever more confident, independent, and sufficient, I had "diamonds on the soles of my shoes."

Oh, the glory of growth; silent, mighty, persistent, inevitable! To awaken, to open up like a flower to the light of a fuller consciousness.
—Emily Carr, Canadian painter and writer (1871-1945)

Finally my circumstances were calming down and my prospects were, for the first time in a very long time, looking up. And indeed, once my change of life passed, my life did change. Through my own intentions and concerted efforts, by constantly questioning and reconfiguring, by struggling to mourn and then release what was irrevocably lost, I was recovering my own misplaced vitality, interest, and energy—and then some. I was beginning to feel the tiniest spark of the exhilarating force that I had been reading about, PMZ or Post Menopausal Zest (a cheery phrase coined by the anthropologist Margaret Mead, who was active well into her seventies), and to believe in the promise of renewed vim and vigor displayed by my women friends and family members who are in their sixth, seventh, eighth, and even ninth decades of life.

By the time I reached my mid-fifties, I was finally ready and able, and for the first time in my life, actually, consciously, conscientiously *willing* to accept the responsibility for my own life and living, and the truth and complete consequences of my own dreams, decisions, and actions. I was a maturing monarch prepared to regulate all of the inner and outer realms of my own domain. At long last, I knew myself to be the uncontested mistress of my own fate. Miraculously, it seemed, I had succeeded in turning my midlife crisis into my crowning achievement. Surely I was a Queen, and not a Crone. I was *The Queen of My Self.*

THE NEW FOUR-FOLD GODDESS MODEL

Contrary to the assumptions of many women, the Triple Goddess model is not universal, nor is it really herstorical. In fact, the paradigm that enjoys so much popularity today is actually not quite as old as I am. It was first articulated in so many words by Robert Graves, a classical scholar, mythographer, and poet, who in his 1948 study, *White Goddess,* synthesized the nine most important early Greek goddesses into three main types. "As Goddess of the Underworld," he writes, "she was concerned with Birth, Procreation, and Death. As Goddess of the Earth she was concerned with the three seasons of Spring, Summer, and Winter: she animated trees and plants and ruled all living creatures. As Goddess of the Sky she was the Moon in her three phases." Summing up the paradigm that many mistakenly believe to be really ancient, he concludes, "As the New Moon or Spring, she was girl; as the Full Moon or Summer, she was woman; as the Old Moon or Winter, she was hag." During the past half century, Graves's definition of three age-identified aspects of a Triple Goddess has worked its way thoroughly into today's huge and diverse Goddess and New Age movements, where it has been wholeheartedly embraced.

Although I have been passionately devoted to the Many Splendored Goddess in Her complex multiplicity for more than thirty years, the Triple Goddess paradigm has never fully resonated with me because it belies what I believe to be the true nature of Nature. The Triple Goddess in all of Her phases is widely understood to represent the complete cyclical wholeness of life. She Who is Three is likened to the moon, the tides, and the seasons, whose mutability She mirrors. And therein lies the rub. After decades of researching, teaching, celebrating, and writing about the cycles of the cosmos and the seasons, I can state unequivocally that the moon has four quarters, not three, and that there are four seasons in the year.

And I guarantee you that the ancients knew this too. Before electrical lighting and air pollution obscured its splendor, the night sky was unimaginably dark and lucid, and the celestial bodies that stood out in vivid contrast to the pitch of the heavens must have been incredibly clear. The spectacular ever-changing sky show provided constant fascination and reverential awe. The moon, especially, was both the source and the recipient of humankind's first religious impulse, and probably the first scientific investigation as well. "The moon, doubtless, is the year, and all living beings," states the *Satapatha-Brahmana*, an ancient Hindu commentary. It is only we moderns who are divorced from celestial awareness and wonderment.

People have lived solely by lunar time for most of our conscious existence and there is ample archeological evidence that the earliest cultures were perfectly aware of the movements and cycles of the moon, which they accurately mapped. A 30,000-year-old piece of bone found in the Dordogne region of France is marked with a series of notches, thought to indicate the lunar cycle. Two similar bones, both about 8,500 years old, unearthed in equatorial Africa and Czechoslovakia, were both incised with repeating sets of fifteen and sixteen notches in precisely ordered intervals, marking the time that transpires between the first sighting of the new crescent moon and the night when the moon attains its fullest circle.

That luminous shape-shifter in space, sometimes slim and sometimes full with light, is at the center of the universal matriarchal mysteries. Starkly silver against the cosmic abyss, the moon is the only luminary in the sky that changes its countenance in a cyclical pattern that is visible to the naked eye. I can imagine our earliest foremothers noting that the moon was always in approximately the same phase each time they bled. Sister moon shared their rhythms, a symphony of fertility composed in thirteen movements, played out in lunar time.

& bleeding
& grazing
& moaning
& chanting
& humming
& drumming the
sounds of the night
—D. H.

Based on my new-found feelings of empowerment, I began to reconsider the Triple Goddess model as it related to my own life, and I started to conceive of a new archetype that seemed to be better suited to the millions of middle-aged women like myself. My new construct of the four stages of a woman's life—Maiden, Mother, *Queen*, and Crone— appeared to be a much more accurate description of the current Way of Womanhood. That there are four stages seems so natural, and in complete metaphoric alignment with the pervasive way that peoples have always ordered existence: the Four Elements, the Four Cardinal Directions of the Earth, the Four Tides and Time Periods of the Day, the Four Quarters of the Moon, the Four Seasons of the Year, and the Four Solstices and Equinoxes of the Calendar.

While the number three signifies a kinship with others in a three-of-a-kind conceptual grouping, such as a family or a holy trinity, four links our lives to that of the planet and defines our relationship with the entire universe. As such, it represents divine order and wholeness. Even now, modern science envisions the universe in four dimensions: length, breadth, width, and time. Because it connects us with the Earth, four is considered to be the most sacred number of tribal peoples everywhere who live in direct contact with the land and the elements of nature.

"There are Four Corners of the Earth that we talk about, the Four Colors of people, and the Four Winds," explains an Algonquin elder, Grandfather William Commanda. "You see the winds—they are spirits." In *The Cherokee Feast of Days*, Joyce Seguiche Hifler writes that "the Elders teach us about the four directions. As we learn about direction, we also learn about attention, about focus, and about power. Each direction has spiritual power." The traditional altar for celebrations of the Day of the Dead, or *Dia de los Muertos*, is four-sided with four levels to represent the four stages of life, the four corners of the Earth, the four seasons, and the four mathematical points upon which the ancient Aztec pyramids were constructed.

The Navajo, too, imbue the number four with extreme holiness. Foursomes permeate the Navajo philosophy and entire way of life. Four sacred directions, four sacred seasons, four sacred moon cycles, four sacred periods of the day, four sacred colors, four sacred original clans, four sacred mountains, four sacred plants, four sacred stones, four sacred seeds, four sacred moments in life, and the evolution of humans through four sacred worlds. They say that just as corn needs sun, air, water, and soil to grow— that is, the four sacred elements of fire, air, water, and earth—people are nourished by four sacred values: Life, Work, Social and Human Relationships, and Reverence and Respect. Their neighbors, the Zia, hold that humans, who play an integral role in the universe, have four sacred obligations: to develop a strong body, a clear mind, a pure spirit, and a devotion to the welfare of all.

In numerology, four represents the generating virtue, the source from which all combinations are possible. It has long been a number of completion, stability, and solidity, considered a perfect number, the root of all things. "Fourfold compositions," writes archeologist Marija Gimbutas, "archetypal of perpetual renewal or wholeness and the moon in the symbolism of Old Europe, are associated with the Great Goddess of Life and Death.... They do not depict the end result of wholeness but rather the continuous striving towards it, the active process of creation."

A woman's work is always toward wholeness.
—May Sarton, American writer (1902-1995)

The figure of a cross, two intersecting lines equal in length and equidistant, arms extended out to touch the four corners of the cosmos, is a universal symbol that was created tens of thousands of years ago in the Neolithic period and is still recognized and widely revered today. The cross was often depicted encased in a circle, a graphic illustration of the four quarters of Earth, the moon, and the seasons, enveloped in the roundness of the expanse of All That There Is. This four-spoked wheel cycles itself endlessly, like Changing Woman, turning, spinning, revolving through time and space. The psychologist Carl Jung viewed another four-fold symbol, the mandala, which illustrates the progression of the seasons of the year and the seasons of our lives through space and time, as a symbol of the Self.

Another variation of the cross is the very ancient four-fold swastika, once held most holy and now vilified beyond redemption. It was used throughout Old Europe and the Mediterranean regions to represent Artemis, Astarte, and Athena. Native American, Hindu, Egyptian, Germanic, and Norse cultures also featured swastika imagery in petroglyphs, pottery, textiles, sand paintings, and ceremonial offerings. In the ancient Minoan civilization of Crete, the swastika was used as a sort of shorthand symbol for the labyrinth, a graphic representation of the journey of life through difficulty and illusion into the cosmic center of enlightenment. With its swinging, swirling arms and legs, the swastika is an evocative symbol of the feminine vortex, a passageway into the center of the consciousness of the world.

Though not common, a number of Goddesses *have* embodied four phases of being. Isis, Mistress of the Four Elements, stands at the center of all existence where Her quadruple energies project through space and time to intersect at that precise point where life is created. Robert Graves's Triple Goddess is associated only with the three elements of earth, air, and water, the three seasons of spring, summer, and winter, and just three phases of the moon—waxing, full, and dark. But Isis ruled all of the forces of nature, including fire, fall, and the waning moon. The Four-Fold Goddess of Eternal Return is the turning of the wheel of life, and She is the road beneath the wheel.

> I am all that
> Is, was or
> Ever will be.
> —Words of Isis inscribed on the
> Temple at Sais, Egypt

The Old Religion of tribal Italy also featured an all-encompassing four-aspected lunar goddess called Tana. As the new moon, She was Diana, the virginal Maiden Goddess, adventurous and daring. As the full moon, She was the Great Round Mother Losna. As the waning moon, She was Manea, the Goddess of the Night Spirits and the departing souls. And as the dark moon She was Umbrea, Goddess of the Underworld, keeper of shadows and secrets and all things hidden. The Aztecs also worshipped a four-part moon goddess called Tlazolteotl, also known as Ixcuina. When the moon was new and waxing, She appeared as a young, brilliant, enticing maiden who was perhaps a bit cruel. When the moon was full, She became a sensuous young woman who loved excitement and lusty pleasures. The waning moon brought Her priestess aspect to the fore. This was Her time to forgive transgressions and bestow blessings of fertility and bounty. As the old dark moon, She was a monster who stole fortunes and ruined lovers.

Hecate, honored as the Greek Triple Goddess, was also called Hecate of the Crossroads for Her role as the divine crossing guard, leading the newly departed souls across the boundary that separates life from death. A crossroad indicates two intersecting paths creating four corners, four quarters. Although Hecate is usually depicted as three-faced: one face looking straight ahead, full front, flanked by two faces in profile, each facing outward, we can imagine Her fourth face looking backward, and thus rendered invisible by the other three—just like the dark fourth phase of the moon when it hides its face from us.

A life-long lover of the moon myself, I live in a constant state of lunar awareness and I attend to the process of my life and living in conscious accordance with the cycle of its four phases. It has long troubled me that so many Triple Goddess models leave out one element, direction, season, or moon phase entirely, and I yearned for the full range of inspiration that can only be offered by the new model of an all-encompassing Goddess of Four Quarters.

As I began integrating my concept of a Four-Fold Goddess into my circles and workshops, women responded with an unexpected passion. Clearly this enthusiastic reception speaks to the need that we feel to find a divine model that truly represents our lives. The Four-Fold Goddess model resonates with our particular circumstances and personal experience and appears to be an authentic archetype for other women today—just as it is for me. I have always said that I practice my religion exactly the way my ancestors did 50,000 years ago. I make it up as I go along. If our spiritual beliefs no longer speak to us, clearly we must change them.

As the model of the Four-Fold Goddess took shape, I developed a new set of correspondences between Her four stages and the four-part moon, the four seasons, elements, directions, and daily periods that made metaphoric sense to me:

Four-Fold Correspondences

Maiden	Mother	Queen	Crone
Waxing Moon	Full Moon	Waning Moon	Dark Moon
Spring	Summer	Autumn	Winter
Water	Earth	Fire	Air
East	South	West	North
Dawn	Noon	Sunset	Midnight

THE MAIDEN, THE MOTHER, THE QUEEN, AND THE CRONE

In the Four-Fold Goddess model I see myself at last. Now, finally, here is an inclusive archetypal Goddess who reflects my existence and those of millions of other women like me. She speaks directly to our development, and Her life changes mirror our own.

The Maiden

Waxing Moon
Spring
Water
East
Dawn

Like the sun and the day with it, the Maiden is born in the east, fresh as dew at dawn. The bringer of the spark of new life from the dark, She is as enthusiastic and hopeful as the promise of any bright morning. The untamed, sometimes unruly, and highly undisciplined spirited vernal nymph who represents the burgeoning potential of life, She is innocent, curious, helpful, and brave. She can also be a brat—puckish, sassy, rebellious, rude, and cruel. She is the waxing moon, opening and filling, expanding Her interests and Her horizons. A young plant in springtime, She is the stalk, the sap, the bud, pushing up and out into the world, making a place for Herself. It is Her role to explore, invent, experiment, learn, and grow. She is a student, intent on self-discovery, expanding Her talents, Her preferences, Her feelings, Her limits—testing Her effect.

Although the direction of east is usually associated with the element of air, and both are most often identified with the Maiden, I see Her as being more suggestive of water. Water represents the emotions, the creative impulses, and the intuitive parts of the brain. Being young, the Maiden is still connected to the deeply spiritual waterways of the unconscious, and has not yet completely subverted the inner voice of our primal brain that "mature" rationality abhors. Free flowing like water, She embodies a fluidity of mind and movement. Her thoughtlessness is both liberating and dangerous. She lives close to the edge of Her emotions and is not yet embarrassed by them, nor does She censure Her feelings.

She is also called the Virgin, not for Her physical chastity, but rather for Her independence of spirit. She is sufficient unto Herself, belonging to no one. She attracts and enjoys love and sexuality, but is not interested in possessing or in being possessed. She has not yet developed the Mother's urge to merge. In her classic work, *Woman's Mysteries: Ancient and Modern,* the psychologist M. Esther Harding writes, "A woman who is a virgin, one-in-herself, does what she does—not because of any desire to please, not to be liked, or to be approved, even by herself; not because of any desire to gain power over another, to catch his interest or love, but because what she does is true." In Her Self-absorption, the Maiden bears Her own divinity.

I am

I am the heart beating wildly
I am the soul blowing across your door
I am the eye straining to see you
I am the lips with nothing to tell
I am the ear and I can hear you
I am the hand knitting wool
I am the foot running for peace and justice
I am the stomach soft and warm
I am the spine stretching with strength
I am the nose quiet and cute
I am the hair flowing in the wind
I am the back walking away
I am the brain filled with knowledge
I am the body mighty and strong
I am me and proudly happy

—Desiree Jackson, 5th grade American student (1992-)

The Mother

Full Moon
Summer
Earth
South
Noon

Mother Summer is the creatrix supreme. She is the full moon, high noon, the apex of sunlight of the year, the fully opened flower, bright and blowsy, flush in Her sexuality and effulgence of spirit. She represents the fullest potential realized, the primal promise of fertility fulfilled. The Mother is earthy, warm, and sensual, steamy like a gorgeous, southern garden abuzz with the need to breed, to mate, to unite, to create, to procreate. She is driven by an undeniable imperative that is a deep rumbling coming from the center of the Earth, the center of Her body, Her womb, Her muse, Her soul. She is fertile ground.

The fat, round Moon Mother is a universal symbol for a full belly, a full pantry, a full purse, a full womb, a full agenda, a full heart, a full life. Biological parent as well as Mother of Invention, She produces and reproduces, making life and culture, love and art. Cosmic creator, nursemaid, caretaker, and provider, She is the farmer who tends Her plots, Her flocks, with patience and care. She is Earth, full with nutriment, committed to the well-being of those around Her, and the daily domestic and productive concerns of the material world are Hers. Less self-absorbed than the Maiden, She labors endlessly to nourish and sustain the fruits of Her passion: Her family, Her job, Her home, Her projects. Endlessly reliable, dependable, solid, and sure, She is the woman whose work is never done.

There is a shadow Mother, too, whose warm, milky southern earthiness and willingness to love has curdled in the tropical midday sun until it is spoiled, sour, stuporous with complacency and laze. Her rock-solid constancy has hardened like petrified wood, leaving Her immovable, intransigent, impenetrable, stubborn, and paralyzed with inertia. Her exquisite caretaking has taken over Her life, causing Her to become bitter, resentful, and martyred. She is the maudlin Mother who sings the "I gave you the best years of my life and I get no thanks" litany. She has reached the point where She has given as much as She can and now needs to mother Herself.

My breasts are huge exciting
amnions of watermelon
your hands can't cup
—*Grace Nichols, Guyanese poet (1950-)*

The Queen

Waning Moon
Autumn
Fire
West
Sunset

The Autumn Queen, who is past Her reproductive years, has never been differentiated in legend from the old Winter Crone, although they are clearly not the same. The Queen, though not yet old, is quite aware that the passing of time is no longer in Her favor. She is not concerned with the business of winding down Her life, however, but rather with living it to the max, before it grows too late. The Queen refuses to go softly into the dark night. She bursts into glorious flame like a dramatic sunset in the western sky, where Her lingering orange and red colors cast a warm assurance over the long evening hours. Dressed in the fabulous splendor of fall foliage, She is ignited with a fiery patina, glowing from within. She is the fire we have been missing.

As the seasons turn, Her focus gets sharper and more concentrated, like the crescent waning moon. To compare the Queen to the waning moon might at first seem negative, implying decay, ebbing, deterioration, and loss. But the energy of the moon is not in decline, nor is it getting smaller in size. The moon is always strong, always full, always brightly reflective. It is only our limited perspective that makes it seem like it is shrinking, darkening, losing its luminous potency, and disappearing into death. The Queen, like the moon past full, concentrates Her wealth of experience. She is committed to honing, toning, distilling, condensing, defining, refining, and honoring Her Self. As She ages, the Queen becomes a rich reduction, infused with the intense bouquet of the flower that She once was, heightened by the fruit that She has become. Like a fine broth or brandy, She is less liquid, more juice.

The Queen of the Crop surveys Her realm and prepares to take in Her Harvest. But before She gathers in the fruits of Her labors, She must create a sturdy receptacle for Her collection of bounty, a vessel worthy of Her own value. Our harvest is more than collecting our due. If we are to survive on what we have produced and grown, we have to do more than simply pick our crops. We have to have ways and means of making the supplies last, preserving them safely for the future. The Queen strives to develop sustainable and renewable strategies and sources of support. She is the Queen of the World, divine director and administrator of resources and systems—Her own and those of society around Her.

Trees are not known for their leaves, nor
even by their blossoms, but by their fruit.
—Eleanor of Aquitaine, French/English Queen
(1122-1204)

The Crone
Dark moon
Winter
Air
North
Midnight

The Winter Crone, who has ridden the wheel of the seasons to completion, is a wizard of transmutation who carries within Her spirit the deep mysteries of life and death and regeneration. She can go into the moonless midnight dark of dark and see the wisdom of the eternal cycle that is sheltered there in the womb/tomb of the universe. Her night vision extends forever, forward and back. She remembers the past and endows the future. She is the holder of knowledge and the repository of culture and civilization. Respected elder, grandmother, griot, shaman, hag, She gathers Her entire community about Her for the telling of stories in the dead of winter, in order to share Her extensive experience for the benefit of all.

The cold arid atmosphere around the Crone has air-dried the fruits of Her life's harvest into hardy leather. She is a tough old broad, Her skin grown thick like hardtack, like jerky or pemmican. While Her body stiffens, Her airy mind, Her spirit, rides the macrocosmic currents of universal truth. She is the Crone of Air, sweeping in from the north in the dark of the moon. She is accompanied by a freezing cold wind, sharp with significance, a terrible swift sword of discernment and clarity that She wields with calculated care—mercilessly, but with great compassion for the larger vision. Like a good gardener, She hews through what is dead, what is unnecessary, what stands in the way of life, the fragile gestating seeds and bulbs and roots of the future. She prunes and trims until She is down to the bones of matter.

When She dies, She lives on through the seeds that She has sown as Maiden, grown as Mother, harvested as Queen, and, ultimately, has Herself created as Crone. She has been, in Her time, bud, blossom, and fruit, and now in Her last cycle, She goes to seed. Her body is the brittle pod, the shell, the husk that breaks open to reveal Her regenerating issue nestled inside. The Crone is also the breeze that disseminates Her seeds, blessing each one with the sacred knowledge of Her age and blowing them a kiss goodbye. She lets them loose into the spiraling airwaves in one final broadcast, sent far and wide, with Her vital message that informs, enlightens, inspires, and ensures the unending cyclical continuation of the species and of the planet.

Our old woman gods, we ask you!
Our old women gods, we ask you!
Then give us long life together,
May we live until our frosted hair
Is white; may we live till then
This life that we now know.
—Tewa Prayer to the Corn Mothers

As I weathered my own midlife passages, the Four-Fold Goddess was born of my need and desire for a divine model whose conditions and changes mirrored my own. Her third aspect, the Queen, became an inspiring mythic mentor for me, representing and embracing as She does an emboldened, empowered, impassioned midlife. Though I conceived of Her, in the end, She taught me, and came to exhibit a forceful persona of Her own, impelling me through the maze of my troubled transformation. The clearer She became as an idea, an image, a guiding archetype in my own life, the more I sensed Her incipient presence in the lives of other women around me. The Queen dwells dormant in each of us. It is up to us to awaken Her with a magical kiss and bring Her to light.

I have found the Goddess in myself and I love her fiercely.
—Ntozake Shange, American poet and playwright (1948-)

Charge of the Queen

I am woman of the sky.
I am woman of the grave.
I am mirror of the moon.
I am reflection of the day.

I am song of the wind.
I am river of the rain.
I am pulse of the stars.
I am churn of the deep.

I am child of the daughter.
I am sister of all sisters.
I am woman of the woman.
I am mother of myself.

I am defender of the beauty.
I am midwife of the change.
I am creator of the vision.
I am lover of it all.

—D. H.

CHAPTER 4

Reigning Monarch

CASTING OFF OUR COCOONS

*And the day came when the risk to
remain tight in bud became more
painful than the risk to bloom.*
—*Anaïs Nin, French writer (1903-1977)*

*U*nlike my grandmother, who personified the archetypal transition from Motherhood to Cronedom at menopause, her daughter, my mother, was a Queen long before her time. Her story is quite a common one now, shared by many millions of women, but in the early 1950s, she was a lonely pioneer when she sought a divorce at the age of forty-five. After nineteen years of homemaking, she was suddenly thrown back into the job market with two kids to raise, no alimony, minuscule child support, and pitifully archaic office skills. As if the situation wasn't challenging enough, she had to endure a fall from suburban grace, the censure and not-so-subtle stigma of being a divorcée. What she *did* have going for her, however, was a mighty determination for a second chance at life—this time on her own terms, thank you very much.

After a few years of acting out of fear, foundering, failing, and starting again from scratch, searching for and finding herself (during which time she miraculously kept us all afloat), my mother finally cast her lot with a start-up land development company in desperate need of her considerable organizational skills. By the time she reached her early fifties, she had worked (and I mean *worked*) her way into a vice presidency of the corporation. The only woman executive, she had a huge budget and hundreds of people in her charge, not the least of whom was herself. She cast herself as a Joan Crawford-Barbara Stanwyck-Rosalind Russell character—a scrappy, independent, smart-as-hell, chic-suited career woman with shoulder pads and an entirely black and white wardrobe—the star of her own version of a 1940s film.

How fortunate I was to have witnessed the process—the struggle, the strain, and the joy—of my mother's midlife transformation from a suffering and subservient wife and unfulfilled PTA mom into a Queen who refused to be invisible, spoke her own mind with authority, and demanded to be heard. The pride and pleasure she derived from her achievements was electrifying, animating her energy and coloring her cheeks with a contagious royal flush. She moved through the world now with confidence in her abilities, and a completely new charisma. With no one to answer to, she was free to pursue her greatest fantasies, long denied. She sold the house and got and decorated the apartment of her dreams. She traveled, took painting and ceramics classes, went to lectures, concerts, the theater, and played cards with her friends, "the girls." She even bought herself a mink coat, a particularly satisfying accomplishment, since, in her day, in her crowd, the husband paid for the furs.

Life loves to be taken by the lapel and told,
"I'm with you kid. Let's go."
—Maya Angelou, American poet (1928-)

Time for a Change

My mother did not get divorced for reasons of adultery or cruelty or even irreconcilable differences, not that her marriage wasn't severely flawed. But her desire to separate actually had little to do with her husband, my father. When that momentous day came, her radical decision was really about her sudden, urgent, and undeniable drive to make her way in the world on her own. Like so many women of her generation, she had graduated directly from her mother's extended household to her own nuclear family, and had no experience of living alone. So, one morning, she simply woke up knowing in her bones that this life that she had not so much chosen, but fallen into nearly two decades ago, was no longer—if it ever was —good for her.

Like my mother, many of us women in our middle years make a complete change in the style and substance of our lives, either out of choice or necessity. Prompted by the stimulation of our internal upheavals and/or by the shifting parameters of our accustomed circumstances, roles, and resources—a newly emptied nest, widowhood, divorce, the death of parents and friends, health issues, the glass ceiling, retirement, regrets, frustration, boredom, curiosity—we are forced to face the sometimes frightening new reality of the present, as well as the future.

Despite the rude awakenings, the unsettling physical and emotional chaos of midlife and all its frightful, presumed ramifications, an amazing number of women find this stage to be the most personally fulfilling and satisfying one of their lives so far. A recent Gallup survey of women aged fifty to sixty-five revealed that fifty-one percent of them feel happier now than they have ever before. This compares to only ten percent who thought the happiest times in their lives were their twenties, seventeen percent who were happiest in their thirties, and sixteen percent who liked their forties best. Just what are we to make of this apparent feeling among so many women that we believe ourselves to be better off once we have lost possession of the very characteristics and trappings that society seems to value most in us—our sexual allure and childbearing capabilities?

The Queen takes up the challenge of change, and with Her eyes wide open She engages in the daunting process of learning who She is now and who She chooses to become. It is important to Her to know that Her thoughts and feelings count, that Her work and interests are meaningful, and that She, Herself, matters. Her growing Self-confidence propels Her to reach for and attain Her own authentic personal power.

I'll walk where my own nature would be leading.
It vexes me to choose another guide.
—Emily Brontë, English writer (1818-1848)

TIES THAT BIND

The Hollywood movies would have us believe that that when men reach their middle years, they become restless in their desire to reclaim their youth. You know the classic plot line, where the successful man throws over his devoted first wife who made his career ascent possible for his nubile, youthful secretary. And they drive off into the sunset in a red Lamborghini convertible, stopping first to refill his prescription for Viagra. Not so. In fact, most midlife marriages are dissolved by the wife for the simple, but very pressing, reason that she needs to be free. Upwards of half of newly divorced middle-aged men seek counseling for their confused and hurt emotions, while only a tiny percentage of women do. While the men scratch their heads and wonder, "What the hell just happened and who is going to cook and match my socks?," the women know perfectly well why they ended the marriage, and consequently, have few second thoughts.

But that doesn't mean we're through with passion. Many women have talked to me about wanting to be—or remain—in an intimate loving relationship, but not wanting to live together as a couple. Some, like Lucia, a forty-six-year-old social worker, reconfigure their marriages and partnerships to accommodate their new emotional requirements for privacy and independence. After her kids moved out and she had extra rooms in her house, she decided that she and her husband should have separate bedrooms. "People feel sorry for me," she laughs. "They assume that something is wrong in our sex lives. But the opposite is actually the case. I love having time alone and a door that I can close for the first time in more than twenty years. My room is my haven and it is exactly the way I want it to be. None of his mess is lying around. And no more snores! It's heaven. When we do have conjugal visits, they are more like dates and have added a huge new excitement to our intimacy."

Others imagine or establish new relationships with new ground rules. "Oh Sam could live across the street," jokes Dee, a fifty-six-year-old college dean. "It would be perfect. He could come over for coffee. We could hang out together. But then I could always send him home when I needed to be alone in order to work or just have some hermit time."

Maria, a pharmaceutical laboratory manager who just turned fifty, recently left her twenty-six-year live-in partnership with another woman. "It was good while it lasted," she says. "We grew up together as a couple, but we also grew apart and I knew that I needed to make a life for myself on my own. I was scared, but I just got my own apartment and I am having a fantastic time creating my own home. Last Friday, I came home from work, poured myself a glass of wine, lit some incense, and put on my favorite jazz CD. I felt so happy, so complete, so fulfilled. It was a real revelation."

The vast majority of women who decide to divorce in midlife are often indifferent to or even cringe at the idea of remarrying. Rather, they are determined to stake their claim on a new life of their own design and choosing without the responsibility or the fealty to a husband. As Carolyn, a sixty-two-year-old accountant, divorced for a decade, puts it, "I enjoy dating, but the minute they leave the toilet seat up or ask me where I've been when I'm not home, it's curtains for them." This desire for living a life of freedom and independence is all the more impressive considering that most women suffer a substantial financial setback after the breakup of a marriage. A marked decline in income apparently makes no difference. You can't put a price on Selfhood.

All the years before, she had lived in a roving and aimless way, and the old love of change came up often to assert its power. Often came back the old longing to live where she would not be bound to anybody—where she might be free, even if she were only free to starve.

—*Lucretia Hale, American writer (1820-1900)*

WORKING IT OUT

During the decades of our Maiden and Motherhood, women grow to meet all of our many demanding responsibilities. Like the moon that gets fuller and fuller with no retreat, we can take on only so much before exploding like a balloon pumped up with too much air. In the second half of Her life, the Queen begins to wane, to contract, to pull in. She opens the air valve and releases what is not to Her benefit. "Perhaps middle age," speculates Anne Morrow Lindbergh, "is, or should be, a period of shedding shells; the shell of ambition, the shell of material accumulation, the shell of the ego. One cannot collect all the beautiful shells on the beach." The Queen rejects the unimportant, the unsupportive, and the inconsequential until She is pared down to the essentials. The purity of Her purpose ever more finely focused, She lives Her life more directly to the point.

When we reach our middle years, we naturally pause and take stock of our lives—our career paths, our goals and aspirations, our sense of meaning. With our perspective on all of the changes and losses that we have seen and suffered, we come to realize that all we have left in our lives is time, and who knows how much of that remains? Therefore, the imperative to live fully, creatively, energetically, effectively, and consciously consumes us. We begin to question—some of us for the first time ever in our good girl lives—all previous assumptions, rules, restrictions, addictions, predictions, and predilections that have ordered our existence. Our heart cries out for authenticity. Is the life that we are living the life that we would choose if we knew that we had only one life to live?

All of the parts of ourselves that we have previously ignored, hidden, sublimated, and suppressed are clamoring for our attention. "What about me?," the career woman yells at the homemaker and the homemaker yells right back, "And what am I, chopped liver? I want my turn, too." "No, it's my turn," demands the daughter, the lover, the wife, the mother. "No, no, look at me," shouts the artist, the writer, the musician, the athlete, the entrepreneur, the adventurer, the healer, the spiritual seeker. An unlived life demands to be lived.

Risk! Risk anything! Care no more for the opinions of others, for those voices. Do the hardest thing on earth for you. Act for yourself.
—Katherine Mansfield, New Zealand writer
(1888-1923)

One therapist I know calls the woman at this decisive stage of midlife "The Dangerous Woman" because she is likely to overthrow all of her previously held notions of responsibility and duty to others, and puts herself—her needs, her desires, her goals, and her dreams—first, despite the repercussions. "Women have to summon up courage to fulfill dormant dreams," writes Alice Walker. When the Queen operates from Her own inner guidance, She releases Her unique gifts and expressions, the sum of Her entire life experience to date, and allows them to ripen and come to fruition. And She recognizes and celebrates the physical, mental, emotional, and spiritual benefits of doing so.

The Queen of Achievement, of Attainment, of Endurance, of Survival has experienced much during Her turns at Maiden and Motherhood. She has traveled to the ends of Her emotions, sometimes willingly, sometimes kicking and screaming. She has explored the depths of the pain and sorrow of the dark times in life, as well as the joys and pleasures of the lightest moments, and has learned and integrated the lessons of each. Her skills are polished, Her confidence high. She is contained, sufficient unto Herself. She knows She can handle whatever might come Her way, because She has, in fact, already done so. She is focused and engaged, fruitful, and a newly fierce champion on Her own behalf. This gives Her clarity of vision and purpose. She knows what She wants and knows She wants it *now*. Her decisions might not make sense to Her friends and family, Her choices might shock and alarm them, but no amount of dissuasion can shake Her from Her resolve. Old doubts and concerns fade in the glaring light of Her determination.

Today, we see many women in public life, ranging the gamut from Hillary Clinton to Sharon Osborne, who have stepped out of the shadows of their husbands and families to pursue their own ambitions. Millions of ordinary women face the same challenge in our daily lives as well. After a couple of decades on the job, many of us feel that we have explored one option or direction as far as we can and now we want to do something else.

Or, we have wanted to do that certain something else all along, but never had the chance, the opportunity, the backing, and/or the nerve to pursue it. Now we recognize that to stay with what we have always done simply by default would be stultifying and self-limiting. And money isn't necessarily the object this time around, either. Now it is more a matter of what is personally satisfying and fulfilling than what is stable or safe.

> *Think like a queen. A queen is not afraid to fail. Failure is another steppingstone to greatnesss.*
> —*Oprah Winfrey, American talk show host, producer, publisher, and actress (1954-)*

A few years ago, when I was in my early fifties, I made the decision after years of procrastinating to begin publishing a quarterly journal on the theme of living in sync with the seasons, a subject that I had been studying, teaching, writing books about, and celebrating for a quarter of a century. It was the next logical intellectual step in my exploration of the cycles of the cosmos and their physical, emotional, and social significance, and this new publication would deal with how to live consciously with the changes of the seasons—including the seasons of our own lives. Good idea or not, however, as my well-meaning friends pointed out, I had no resources to support this ambitious project. But I was beyond reason, my biological clock was ticking, though I wasn't thinking of babies. Mortality was on my mind—mine. If I didn't do this now, when would I?

Needless to say, I didn't listen to the criticism, constructive though it might have been, and I went right on ahead with my plan. And, yes, they were right. But though I incurred a very large debt as a result, I have no regrets. Publishing the journal has been a most rewarding endeavor, a four-times-a-year discipline that challenges me to stay in tune with and respond to the times, even as they change. This effort keeps me alert and in the moment—a worthy lesson at any price. Today, after six years, *Always in Season: Living in Sync with the Cycles* is still publishing and has loyal subscribers in thirty-one states and eight countries who are not simply readers but more like an extended community of like-minded souls, a network of support, an international circle of care and concern. Surely this is what truly matters.

At this point in our lives, many women have struggled mightily to advance their careers and are now beginning to reap the rewards. Florinda, a nurse's aide in the hospice where my foster son is living out his last days, came to New York as a young woman from the Caribbean and took a job that was meant to be temporary until she could go to nursing school. Alas, as so often happens with the best-laid plans, life intervened. She became pregnant and after her first child was born, several more followed. Her man left her without any financial help, her mother fell ill, and before she knew it, she was solely responsible for the care and feeding of five other people. But no matter how difficult her life seemed, how many bedpans she emptied or diapers she changed, she remained firm in her dedication to the healing arts. As her children grew older and less dependent, she began to take classes in nursing, gradually working her way toward her goal. And now, with her kids all in college and her mother having passed on, she is finally, after twenty-five years of trying, within a few credit hours of achieving her childhood dream. This is a woman who holds her head very high indeed. Queenly, one might say.

I am independent. I can live alone and I love to work.
—*Mary Cassatt, American painter (1844-1926)*

For other women, the time and energy-consuming pursuit of career is now thrown into an unexpected light. With the advent of her fiftieth birthday, Lucinda, an internationally-known sculptor, realized that the life she had been leading for thirty years as a single, driven, professional woman no longer fulfilled her. She had accomplished all of the goals with which she had begun and was now bored and emotionally drained by the stressful pitch of the art world. Plus, she had just gone a round with cancer, losing her left breast in the struggle. As part of her recovery process, she reevaluated her priorities and realized that they were lopsided. She understood that she wanted more emotional connection and stability in her life and that now—or never—was the time to experience the challenges and pleasures of a domestic, familial existence. So she adopted a baby and settled in to raise her.

One of my clients, Jean, also decided to shift her focus inward after her twenty-six-year career as an elementary school teacher had left her physically and emotionally exhausted. Even though she was a widow with no means of support other than her salary, and dependent on her pension to support herself in old age, she quit her job four years before the official retirement age, cutting her benefits in half. Her friends were horrified at her impetuousness and worried about her future. "But I was tired and bored, and I just didn't want to do this any more. It was dragging me down. It didn't seem worth it to hang on," she explained. "Then my last child got married and I turned sixty and that did it for me. I was *out* of there," she told me with a glint in her eye when I met her four years later.

Now, at sixty-four, she is radiantly happy with the changes that she has dared to make. While she is proud of her accomplishments, she is even more proud of her newly discovered courage. She still doesn't quite believe that she actually had the guts to quit a sure thing and commit herself to an uncertain fate with nothing and no one to depend on but herself. But after some casting about, she learned that she could combine her extensive experience as an educator with her life-long love of reading and writing, and she is now teaching journal writing and oral history to senior citizens. "It was just like my entire life was leading up to this," she told me with pride. "I wish I had been doing this all along." But without her own life experience, she would not have the same depth of understanding of the lives of her elderly students.

Avoiding danger is no safer in the long run than outright exposure. Life is either a daring adventure, or nothing.
—Helen Keller, American humanitarian (1880-1968)

Other women stay on the same professional course for decades and never grow stale, but improve and refine our talents as we go. Our interest doesn't flag when we know ourselves to be on the true path of pursuing our life's calling. In these cases, the older and wiser we grow, the wider our spheres of influence become, allowing us to make a real difference in the world. My old friend, Mona, had also been a teacher for decades—in her case for more than thirty years—and she maintains that there was never a day that she wasn't thrilled with her vocation. For years she had fought off offers and sometimes outright pleas to become an assistant principal, but she resisted the temptation of increased status and a bigger salary. She knew what she was good at and what she loved.

Then, last year, she accepted a position with the powerful United Federation of Teachers union, a job that would enable her to create policy for improving the quality of education for children and of work conditions for teachers. Though she is out of the classroom now, she believes her effectiveness as an educator is vastly expanded and is the crowning achievement of her career. She had worked diligently at what she loved for years, never compromised, and ultimately reached an unhoped-for height of attainment and authority, not to mention a corner office, a serious salary, and a deeply satisfying affirmation of her abilities. On achieving her success at midlife, she says, "You know the story of the tortoise and the hare? Well, I was the tortoise and I won in the end."

And, finally, some of us seek to rediscover earlier aspirations and talents that were somehow abandoned along the roadside during our life's journey. As her body started to experience the changes of midlife, Audrey, a student of mine, remembered how strong and fast she had been in her youth and began feeling resentful that she had been forced by her father as a young girl to abandon her athletic abilities and proclivities, her very substantial physical prowess, in the interest of becoming more ladylike. When she hit fifty, Audrey decided to dedicate herself to the rediscovery and reclamation of her own body.

Tired of feeling like a victim, aggrieved, wronged, robbed of physical success, she accepted the challenge and explored ways to express her long-suppressed athletic interests. She took up weights, tennis, Pilates; she indulged in massages, acupuncture, and other physical therapies. In short, she took back her body, her power, and her control. Audrey recently confided that turning fifty has been great for her, because she had never before in her life experienced her body in such a positive way and at the same time been so in touch with her inner desires. She is, at long last, fit for a Queen.

What distinguishes these midlife women is that they acted with purpose and tenacity to further their own needs and desires as well as those of the greater good. Their courage in trying circumstances does not mean that they were not afraid, but that they did not let their fear stop them from doing what they felt must be done. Instead of depending on someone or something else to take care of business—a knight in shining armor, a successful husband, a doting parent, the class system, law and order—they rolled up their sleeves and did what they knew needed doing. They took up the sword, the pen, the struggle, the cause, the responsibility, themselves.

Never apologize, never retreat, never explain.
Get the thing done and let them howl.
—Nellie McClung, Canadian suffragist and writer
    (1873-1951)

QUEENS THROUGH THE AGES

The mighty Queen, the great and wise, brave and compassionate woman ruler, the reigning commander of Her domain, is an expansive, expressive, accessible, energetic archetype who represents a mature female power, authority, responsibility, and influence worthy of our emulation. There have always been exceptional Queens, royal and otherwise—inspiring and motivating examples of monarchs, matriarchs, amazons, fabulous furies, sheroes, and prominent leaders from all cultures and walks of life—to serve as role models for those of us who are striving to mold ourselves in Her image of sovereignty and strength.

Among the Hopi people, women and men are not considered to be completely grown-up adults until they have reached their mid-fifties at least. Women who are not yet fifty are not thought to be mature enough to participate in the weightier matters of ceremony. Despite however accomplished they might be, how responsible, how many children they do or don't have, their wisdom is not yet not believed to be completely developed. They are considered still too involved in the practical matters of life and living, too distracted and preoccupied to be in attunement with Spirit —and thus their power. Many cultures believe that a menopausal woman retains inside her body the blood that she used to shed each month. This blood that she preserves for herself is the fire-red source of her potency. The French have a saying that when women lose their blood, they gain their voice.

The Matriarch Queen is not afraid to speak Her truth. She has kept Her power a hidden secret, held fast just below the surface, the lid screwed on tight to prevent an accidental boil-over. Now, She burns with the passion and the power of a dormant volcano finally let loose from the intolerable internal pressure borne for so long. The fires of Her impatience have burned away all the underbrush and now She can see the forest for the trees. Knowing through Her personal experience what is true and valuable, and having learned, usually the hard way, to be proactive, She pledges Her royal Self to defend and promote all that is precious. Fired by righteous indignation at the wrongs of the world, the Amazon Queen takes on the responsibility of Her authority with fervor and command.

When, in the first century AD, the Romans invaded her tribal lands in old Britain, the Celtic Queen Boudicca organized a massive general uprising by tens of thousands of men and women from different tribes in a united rebellion against the occupying forces of the Roman Empire. Boudicca's armies succeeded in capturing and reclaiming London, Colchester, and St. Albans, major cultural centers that had been Romanized. "It will not be the first time, Britons, that you have been victorious under the conduct of your queen," she proclaimed. "For my part, I come not here as one descended from royal blood, not to fight for empire or riches, but as one of the common people, to avenge the loss of their liberty, the wrongs of myself, and my children." Though the peasant insurrection was ultimately lost and the rebel troops were slaughtered, Queen Boudicca escaped with her daughters. In the end, they poisoned themselves rather than allow themselves to be captured, but the result of her campaign was, while not freedom, a more lenient Roman regime.

We are not interested in the possibilities of defeat.
—Victoria, English Queen (1819-1901)

In twelfth-century Germany, at a time when women's roles were heavily circumscribed, the Abbess Hildegard of Bingen found extraordinary ways to express her talents. Born of nobility, Hildegard was raised and educated from the age of seven by the Benedictine nuns. At the age of forty-three, she became abbess of her community. In addition to her extensive spiritual and administrative responsibilities, she managed to pursue and excel at a mind-boggling array of disciplines. She was a visionary, theologian, prophet, exorcist, healer, natural historian, hagiographer, founder of two monasteries, correspondent, confidante, political advisor to kings and popes, poet, performer, author of the world's first morality play, creator of a new language and alphabet, and composer of chants rich in mystical imagery and florid musicality that are popular even today. A devotee of the feminine side of God, she once received a vision that counseled her, "Therefore pour out a fountain of abundance, over-flow with mysterious learning, so that those who want you to be despicable on account of Eve's transgression may be overwhelmed by the flood of your profusion."

But perhaps nowhere in history were women held in higher standing and regard than in Mama Africa, the birthplace of humanity and the world's first great civilizations, with its preponderance of matrilineal societies. "You know that in our country there were even matriarchal societies where women were the most important element," writes Amilcar Cabral, the Guinean leader of the African Liberation Movement, in *Return to the Source*. "They were not queens because they were the daughters of kings. They had queens succeeding queens. The religious leaders were women, too."

Probably the most famous woman in African history is Queen Nzinga Mbande, Queen of the N'dongo and Matamba in West Africa, who ruled Angola for thirty-some years in the mid-1600s. In 1621, at the age of thirty-nine, she negotiated with the Portuguese for the preservation of Angolan independence while seated on the back of a kneeling servant, an ingenious and face-saving performance, as the colonialists had not provided a chair for her in an attempt to embarrass and humiliate her. Years later, Nzinga refused to hand back runaway slaves to the Portuguese, thus bringing down their colonial wrath. Along with her female officers and advisors, Nzinga formed formidable tribal alliances and gathered a vast army that, in true guerrilla fashion, harassed the Portuguese to exhaustion from all sides while avoiding direct confrontation. Politically astute, she formed alliances with other foreign powers, pitting them against one another to free Angola of European influence.

Queen Nzinga was a visionary political leader, competent and self-sacrificing, completely devoted to the resistance movement against the European slave traders. She possessed an abundance of both steely hardness and soft charm and used each, depending on the situation, as a tactical tool when it suited her. Her death in 1663 left her people vulnerable to the massive Portuguese slave trade. Yet her struggle against it helped to inspire others to follow in her powerful path and continue to mount offensives against the White invaders. Queen Nzinga is so revered that, despite logic, a pre-historic imprint of what looks to be a foot on a rock at Pungu Andongo in Angola is said to be hers.

One of Queen Nzinga's spiritual children, a ferocious middle-aged woman known as Nanny, led a victorious slave revolt in Jamaica in the 1720s, then founded a free Maroon community called Nannyville. It is said that when the pursuing British fired cannonballs into their village, Nanny caught them between her buttocks and shot them right back at the soldiers. Harriet Tubman, another woman on Queen Nzinga's mission, was, in addition to being the famous founder of the Underground Railroad, a soldier in the Union army of the North. On June 2, 1863, at the age of sixty-six, she led a mission on the Tennessee River with three gunboats under her command. Queen Harriet and her allies blew up a Confederate bridge, engaged in espionage, and saved the lives of seven-hundred and fifty-six slaves. After the war, the army not only refused to recognize her contributions, but also robbed her of her veteran's pension.

There have been notable Queens in more recent times as well. Eleanor Roosevelt, a shy, self-conscious, and naturally retiring woman, was thrust feet first into the limelight when she became First Lady of the United States in 1933 at the age of forty-eight. Though this new role was extremely painful for her, rather than allowing herself to be intimidated by public life, she consciously chose to use her visibility and enormous influence to further the causes of social justice in which she so firmly believed. She became an outspoken crusader for the rights of the oppressed, a self-imposed rule that lasted long after her tenure in the White House, and she remained an active advocate for equality, peace, and freedom for the rest of her life. "You must do the thing you think you cannot do," she later declared. "You gain strength, courage, and confidence in every experience in which you really stop to look fear in the face."

Following this dictum, in 1955 Rosa Parks, a forty-two-year-old seamstress, sat down in the front of the bus in Birmingham, Alabama, and refused to relinquish her seat to a white man when the driver ordered her to move. The popular legend says that she was tired after a hard day's work, and her feet hurt. No doubt, but surely her feet had ached for years. It seems to me that she had simply reached a now-or-never-point in her life where she was willing to accept the awesome responsibility for defending herself, for demanding to be treated with the dignity and respect that she knew she deserved—come what may. Her life, indeed the life of the entire nation, was never to be the same. What resulted from her spontaneously courageous act was nothing less than the legal equality of the races, which was probably the furthest thing from her mind that fateful day. But when a Queen stands up to opposition or oppression in any form and speaks her truth out loud, she steps into her sovereignty and there is no turning back.

> *They tell me nothing but lies here, and they think they can break my spirit. But I believe what I choose and say nothing. I am not so simple as I seem.*
> —*Catherine of Aragon, Spanish Queen of England (1485-1536)*

FROM THIS DAY FORTH

Like these remarkable women, after an inevitable midlife transition period of feeling lost, confused, and without control of Her destiny, the Queen finally takes charge. She steps up to the situations of Her life and takes back the reins of Her power. Or not.

Becoming a Queen is not automatic, nor is it instantaneous. Unlike dynastic royalty, where the only path to the throne is through inheritance or marriage, the archetypal Queen of Her Self must earn Her own crown. As Simone de Beauvoir, the French philosopher and feminist said, "One is not *born* a woman, one *becomes* one." So, how does one become a Queen?

In order to qualify for Queendom, we must choose to lay claim to the mighty power of self-determination and free will. A Queen is not a grownup princess gliding through life swathed in a protective sheath of entitlement. Rather, She must struggle for and earn Her authority and respect. We can step into our sovereignty only if we actually embrace it, embody it, employ it, enjoy it, and make it fully our own by conscious intent and conscientious effort. There is no such thing as Queen for a Day.

> *I went in through the doors of the treasury of wisdom, and I drew for myself the waters of understanding. I went into the blaze of the sun's flame, and it lighted me with its splendor, and I made of it a shield for myself.*
> —Makeda, Queen of Sheba
> (Tenth Century BC)

CHAPTER 5

The Queen and I

EMBRACING HER MAJESTY

*You need only to claim the events of your life
to make yourself yours. When you truly
possess all you have been and done, which
may take some time, you are fierce with reality.*

—*Florida Scott-Maxwell, American/Scot
psychologist and writer (1884-1968)*

When I started introducing the Queen in workshops and articles as a helpful archetype for midlife women, I received many requests for detailed instructions on how to become a Queen. "Dear Mama Donna," women would write, "I want to be a Queen, too. How do I access my power? How can I feel good about myself? How do I change my life? How do I find magic and spiritual wisdom? How do I know what to do? How do I learn how to rule?" The reality is that I cannot possibly know how anyone else will attain her Queendom, I only know how I came into mine, and that is largely through hindsight. The truth, my truth at least, is that there is no one truth. We must each find our own way in this world. As a shaman, I teach through example, but not through dictum. I can and do offer information, exposure, personal experience, encouragement, inspiration, suggestions and support to my constituents, but I cannot—dare not —pass judgment or establish rules and laws. It is simply not for me to say.

My students and clients often come to me for help and spiritual guidance. When they do, I listen to their concerns and embrace their needs. I pat them on the back, give them a good swift kick in the butt, or let them cry on my shoulder, as needed. I can tell them what I did in such and such situation, how I did it, what I learned from this or that lesson, but I cannot tell them what they should do. Only they know what they know. What I can do is aid them in reaching into the well of their own deepest wisdom, and help them to hear the messages from their best inner Selves. A woman who has attended several of my workshops recently hugged me and told me that I had changed her life. "Well, no, of course I didn't, honey," I assured her. "You changed your own life." The fact of the matter remains that I could not give her what was not already hers.

TAKING CHARGE

Each one of us has a story, a myth, a legend to write, to paint—and to live. The shamanic principle with which I operate is that every person has her own mission in this lifetime: her own path, her own dreams, her own symbols and sensibilities, her own visions and designs, her own way of learning, her own personalized hard-won lessons. That we each have a singular life to live. That every one of us must figure out for ourselves the fullest, richest, most effective, ethical, and satisfying way in which to do it; and moreover, that each and every one of us possesses the wisdom, the power, and the responsibility to make it so.

*You take your life in your own hands, and
what happens? A terrible thing: no one to blame.*
—Erica Jong, American writer (1942-)

The story of our lives is ours to create. We can design our own roles and ideals, compose the scripts, and author the sagas of our own futures and that of the environment around us. While we cannot necessarily control the circumstances and influences that present themselves to us in the course of living, we can choose how we will respond to them when they do arise. Our power of choice is our sole control in the world. With each new paragraph, each turn of the page, each blink of the eye, each new dawn, each moment in time, we are gifted with another opportunity to exercise our right to choose. Coffee or tea? Lemon or milk? Right or left? Stairs or elevator? Vacuum? Vote? Cheat? Trust? Care? Dare? Change? What paths we take, what decisions we make, influence how the story will proceed and who we will be from this day forth.

The difficult times that we encounter in our lives might tempt us to dull our senses and opt out of any upsetting experiences, choosing not to let things "get to us." We often try to ignore the hard parts—pain, fear, guilt, grief, confusion, anger, and disappointment—dilute their impact, drown them out in an endless list of pleasurable addictions: soporifics, anesthetics, mood enhancers, caffeine, food, hormones. We can even turn ourselves off altogether. The point is we don't *have* to engage in the emotional upheaval of life. Nobody is making us. We could choose to drink cabernet and watch public television, play cards, play it safe, every night for the rest of our lives if we wanted to. It *is* an option. It is ultimately up to us whether we succumb to the unexamined life or try to figure out what the hell is going on inside us and around us, and engage in it, alter, change, and grow with it, so that we might fulfill our greatest destiny and dreams.

I postpone death by living, by suffering,
by error, by risking, by giving, by losing.
—Anaïs Nin, French writer (1903-1977)

At midlife, we are at a major crossroads in our lives, and we can choose to move ahead, turn right or left, stay where we are, or go back where we came from. The Queen chooses always to choose, to involve Herself fully in the process of Her life and living, and to actively direct the drama of Her myth. She urges us take up the challenges of changing, of aging, engaging in all that life has to offer. And She reminds us to look upon the difficulties, disruptions, disappointments, fears, and failures we have experienced as important life lessons, without which we could never hope to ascend to a throne of responsibility and rule. She encourages us to entertain the entire palette of our emotions, for there is where we find our strength and knowledge and true value. Some things in life just have to be learned the hard way and evading them is counter-productive and eventually destructive. The only way to *get through* them is to *go through* them. There is a wonderful old African-American Spiritual that says, "So high, you can't get over it. So low, you can't get under it. So wide you can't get around it. You gotta go through the door."

And supposing you have tried and failed again and again,
you may have a fresh start any moment you choose,
for this thing we call 'failure' is not the falling down,
but the staying down.
—*Mary Pickford, Canadian-born American Actress*
(1893-1979)

STEPPING INTO SOVEREIGNTY

Coming from the tough love school of spiritual counseling as I do, I feel that it is only fair to warn you, *there are no 10 easy steps to sovereignty.* The roads leading to Queendom are diverse and many. The way to Self-esteem can be complicated and long. Each woman must take her own path, make her own trail, clear a passage for herself through the thick brambles that reach up to trip her. What roads do exist are unmapped, bumpy, and full of potholes, tumbleweed, and road-kill. There are no shortcuts along the Queen's Highway, no services, no shoulders, no signage, but many detours and cul-du-sacs. And the fare can be exorbitant. As Abigail Van Buren, the originator of the syndicated column, "Dear Abby," once noted, "If we could sell our experiences for what they cost us, we'd be millionaires." Like any grand journey, the trip toward self-dominion requires stamina, determination, and the passionate desire to travel. But if we pack properly, check our tires frequently, and take time for picnics, the adventure is incomparable. And the destination of Self-empowerment is majestic.

The Queen chooses to engage Her Self despite the difficulties.

The Self, according to Carl Jung, is the center, the midpoint of the personality, the crossroads where our personal and collective conscious and unconscious processes intersect. The Self encompasses the totality of who we are. It is, he writes, "a kind of central point within the psyche to which everything is related, by which everything is arranged, and which itself is a source of energy. The energy of the central point is manifested in the almost irresistible compulsion and urge to *become what one is*, just as every organism is driven to assume the form that is characteristic of its nature, no matter what the circumstances." The Self is the sum of all of our parts, and holistically, it is greater than the sum of all of our parts. The fluid Self transcends time and space, expanding and shape-shifting, changing and adapting to accommodate the possibility of all possibility.

In the art and philosophy of many cultures, the nature of the Self is represented by a four-part symbol such as a mandala, a labyrinth, an equilateral cross, a swastika, or a four-leaf clover. These symbols mirror the four-partite systems that organize the totality of the cosmos into the four seasons of the year, the four phases of the moon, the four cardinal directions. The Four-Fold Goddess is representative of not only the stages and ages of a woman's life, She also stands for the four parts that comprise our united Self. The Self, the Soul, the Center of a person is commonly thought to include our physical, mental, emotional, and spiritual sides. These aspects are the ways in which we perceive and relate to the world around us and to our inner selves as well. Jung calls these aspects "functions," and identifies them as sensing (physical), thinking (mental), feeling (emotional), and intuiting (spiritual). These four parts combine to compose our outlook and our insight. Together, they constitute our unique ways and means of being.

Our Queenly assignment, should we choose to accept it, is to identify, understand, and connect all the component parts of ourselves, to attempt to develop and balance them equally, and to maintain them all in good working order. The Self is like a jigsaw puzzle or a quilt that promises to become a beautiful whole if we spend the necessary time and concentration to assemble it. It is at once the puzzle, the parts of the puzzle, and also, most importantly, the process of piecing them together. The ideal of the Queen inspires us to design the artful patchwork of our own lives, pieced together from the wild and wonderful patterns of our own personality and experiences, and crafted from our individual inner authority. Once we do, we are able to shift into a new stage of life, a new state of being, a renaissance, ready to rule.

The Self is the seat of sovereignty of the Queen. It is Her throne and Her domain, at once Her base of power and Her field of operation. Stepping into our sovereignty involves an almost alchemical process of adding, extracting, refining, combining, and recombining the myriad elements that make up our four parts in the constantly evolving effort of perfecting the power of our best Selves. The holy elixir that we seek is the transformation of the painful, rejected, neglected, wounded, unsatisfied, unsatisfactory parts of the Self, into the unified, organized, energized, golden glory and grace of the fulfilled Queen. It is through our sincere and complete participation in this process that we learn how to recognize, claim, and proclaim our own true power. The power of the fully engaged Self.

The Queen's Rules of Engagement:
There are no rules.
There is only our best Intention
and our conscientious Attention.

There are no rules, no recipes, no prescriptions, no instruction manuals, no precise formulas to follow when it comes to pursuing the daunting process of Stepping into Sovereignty. This does not, however, mean that anything goes. Just as in life itself, everything counts. Every single solitary thing that we do or don't do, think or don't think, matters. This is the bottom line of our responsibility—to ourselves and to others. Our Intentions have to be perfectly pure and our Attention to the details of our process has to be focused and disciplined, and in exact alignment with our Intentions. The quality of our engagement needs to be really right, not according to the standards of anyone else, but only according to our own inner truth.

Far away there in the sunshine are my highest aspirations.
I may not reach them, but I can look up and see their
beauty, believe in them, and try to follow where they lead.
—Louisa May Alcott, American writer (1832-1888)

Clearly, the purity of our Intention and Attention assures that there can be no cheating or cutting of corners in our search for inner wisdom and power. What would be the point? We would only be short-changing ourselves. When we commit to engaging in the process of our own transformation, the search for our inner wisdom, the development of our Self-esteem, the elevation of our status and standing, we are consciously choosing to accept total cause-and-effect accountability for our own lives and living. And since the decision to pursue our personal sovereignty is ours and ours alone, made with clear Intention and without outside direction or duress, we must own our process. Our Attention must be unimpeachable, our attitude positively impeccable.

The Queen's Attitudes of Engagement:
Self-Defense
Self-Discipline
Self-Devotion
Self-Determination

The Queen is firm in the Defense of Her time, Her space, Her boundaries, Her priorities, Her preferences, Her ethics, Her needs, Her desires, Her safety, and Her sense of well-being. Her Self-Defense is not defensive, however. She acts not from the feeble uncertainty of a victim, but from the steady and stable center of Her acceptance and ownership of Her own thoughts and feelings, beliefs and actions. She is sure of Her Self. The Queen allows Herself to feel worthy, entitled, and esteemed based on the success of Her own efforts, accomplishments, and growth. Her Intention is to learn and master all of the ways that She can feed, feel, help, heal, hear, change, mend, befriend, embrace, and love Her Self. She takes care of Herself on every level. And She vehemently defends Her right to do so.

The Queen also exerts Her considerable sense of Self-Discipline to allow Herself only those thoughts and deeds that promote positive possibilities. She purposefully surrounds Herself with influences that affirm Her Intentions and Attentions: people, places, things, and ideas that are inspiring, uplifting, and life-affirming. She assesses the circumstances of Her life, takes responsibility for them, and banishes Her bad habits of body, mind, emotion, and spirit that prevent Her from progressing. The Queen reflects, selects, and rejects, objectively editing and discarding what no longer serves Her, releasing what She no longer needs. She thus streamlines and distills Her belongings, Her body, and Her mental and emotional baggage, lightening Her load so that She might move ahead unimpaired.

As the Queen embarks on the process of Stepping into Sovereignty, She maintains a practice of daily Self-Devotion. She displays a loyal attachment, commitment, affection, reverence, and respect toward all of life—including Her own. Her Intention is to honor the wisdom, diversity, changeability, energy, strength, beauty, creativity, and power that She sees in Her Self, in the same way and with the same devotion and dedication that She offers to Mother Earth. And She diligently tries to accord Herself the same amount and degree of loving attention. She does this by choosing to "Be Here Now" in each precious moment, fully engaged in the process of Her life with a genuine enthusiasm, a concentrated awareness, a passionate participation, and a sacred trust. The Queen recognizes Her many blessings and is thankful for even Her hardest lessons, practicing a profound attitude of gratitude.

The Queen is Determined to be Self-Determined. She stands on Her own feet, and stands Her ground when challenged. She chooses to take the ambitious journey, the long weary road to discover and empower Her inner wisdom and spirit, Her sovereign Self. Her decision is informed and well intentioned, and She accepts the daunting responsibility for Her difficult and demanding choice. As exhausting as the trip might be, She is single-minded in Her Determination, resolute and unwavering in Her Devotion, Discipline, and Defense of Her Intentions and Attentions. She cannot be stopped. Nothing silences Her sense of truth. She makes sure that Her voice is heard, Her opinions are known, Her needs and desires, regarded.

WE KNOW WHAT WE KNOW

Although the Queen is an excellent role model and source of inspiration, we don't need a teacher or a guru to tell us what we should do for our Self-development, or how we need to change and grow. Each of us knows perfectly well what is right for us. Informed by the four parts of our being—physical, mental, emotional, and spiritual—we know in our gut, our mind, our heart, and our soul when something is right, because it *feels* right. And when something feels wrong, we certainly know that, too. The answers to our confusion and questions, our yearnings and longings, are right here inside of us where we keep them safe and warm—perhaps too safe, hidden secretly away in the corners of dark caves, far away from our own prying eyes.

*It always comes down to the same necessity: go deep
enough and there is a bedrock of truth, however hard.*
—*May Sarton, American writer and poet (1912-1995)*

Our lessons, and our understanding of them, are often not immediately available or obvious to us. They often come encoded in signs and symbols that seem like a foreign language. But, no matter how difficult, it is up to us to access them if we dare. If we care to earn our sovereignty, we must excavate the buried treasure of our own value and infinite worth. Our coming into power depends upon it. If we do take up the challenge to explore and mine the depths of our Selves, we will discover the unexpected caverns of courage, phosphorescent pools of passion, and glittering, crystal-rich veins of gem-like wisdom running through their passages and crevices. All we need are the right tools to get at them, extract them, and polish them. And I don't know about you, but nobody ever told me that it was going to be easy.

The Queen's Tools of Engagement:
Consolation
Contemplation
Seclusion
Creation

The tools we need to step into sovereignty are available for us under the guidance of the Queen, Herself, who offers a steady supply of handy, helpful, healing devices to ease and refine our labors as we search for our true Selves. These trusty tools are instruments that facilitate growth, change, and transformation in every aspect of our personality, corresponding to the four directions, seasons, tides, and elements. The Queen, too, displays four aspects of Her being, which we recognize in the physical, mental, emotional, and spiritual dimensions of Herself.

I've found a wonderful metaphor for these four dimensions of the Queen in the Tarot cards, an old and widespread system of divination. We use the symbols of the Tarot to illuminate the changes and concerns in our own lives, to suggest hidden meanings and possible solutions. Each of the four suits in a deck is under the protection of a different aspect of the Queen, Mistress of Her particular realm.

The Four Aspects of the Tarot Queens

Disks	Swords	Cups	Wands
Physical	Mental	Emotional	Spiritual
Sensing	Thinking	Feeling	Intuiting
Earth	Air	Water	Fire
Consolation	Contemplation	Seclusion	Creation
Defense	Discipline	Devotion	Determination
Gather In	Throw Out	Go In	Reach Out
Sanctify	Articulate	Identify	Actualize
Receive	Conceive	Believe	Achieve

The Queen of Disks symbolizes mastery of the physical, material plane. She uses Consolation to support and cosset Herself in the same manner in which She has served others. The Queen of Swords wields the sharp blade of the lessons of the mind. She employs Contemplation—Her airy mental focus, conscious and subconscious both—to enable Her to make connections, distinctions, and choices. The Queen of Cups holds the keys to the emotional realm. She depends on Seclusion to help Her lose and then find Herself in the vast expanses of Her watery feelings. The Queen of Wands harnesses the power of Creation, to fire the rockets of Her spirit. Jet-propelled, She flies into the furthest reaches of Her spiritual Self.

THE QUEEN'S HIGHWAY

So, here we are, about to embark on our grand adventure into the wilderness in search of our mature Selves. We have done our research, made our preparations, trained our bodies, and packed our bag with all the appropriate tools. Our attitude is positive and earnest, Self-devoted, Self-disciplined, Self-defended, and Self-determined to make the best of this huge transition in our lives. We are frightened by what pitfalls we might encounter, and are thrilled with the anticipation of the great riches that we hope to find. On your mark. Ready. Set. Go!

———————

I have always had a dread of becoming a passenger in life.
—Margrethe 11, Queen of Denmark (1940-)

The Queen Suggests:
A Consideration Upon Departure

Before we leave, it would seem fitting to set our Intentions and focus our Attention for the journey ahead.

Identify your Intention. Know your destination. And know that one destination usually leads to another on the journey of life. Some destinations are crossroads, traffic circles, or travel hubs.

Where are you now?
Where are you coming from?
Where are you heading?
Why are you traveling?
Do you want the fastest way or the scenic route?
What are you taking with you?
What are you leaving behind?

Take the time and trouble to figure out what you are looking for—in the short term and for the future.

Articulate your Intention. Be as precise as you can about what you want. This is important because by imagining and clarifying your desires and Intentions, you are sending the energy to attract them to you.

If you can name it, you claim it
If you can see it, you can be it.

Sanctify your Intention. Remind yourself of what you are doing and why. Pledge your allegiance to doing it. Inscribe it in your notebook, make a painting or collage of it, sing it to yourself in the shower, compose poetry and affirmations to inspire you to achieve it, create an altar dedicated to the pursuit of it. Light a candle to bless yourself as being worthy of the means and ends of it.

Actualize your Intention. Devote your thorough Attention to all the details that are required to make your Intention a reality.

Follow through.
Do what needs to be done.
Don't give up.

The Queen of Disks chooses Consolation.
With comfort and compassion, She cares
for Her Self: body, mind, heart, and spirit.

Once we have gotten in touch with and gained mastery of our Intentions, it is time to turn our Attention to the physical, material aspect of our being. In our renewed sense of Self-interest, we need to redirect back into ourselves some of the love and strength that we give so freely to others. Now with our plans conceived and coalesced, the worst of our hard times past, and our triumphs secured, it is crucial that we nurture our bodies as well as our most precious dreams, and lavish upon ourselves an endless flow of emotional and spiritual sustenance and physical care. Though our Intentions are formed by our mental, emotional, and spiritual functions, we must carry them through on the physical/material plane. Our bodies, after all, must be able to carry the energy of our goals and sustain us through the long haul.

Earthbody, brief spouse, what a strangely
inconvenient marriage. Yet you are my only
true support. And though you may never
fathom what I secretly am, may you—
who accepted the nature of existence itself—
stay with me in your lovely halo of death
till I depart, dearest Body, my slave, my queen.
—Janine Canan, American poet (1942-)

The Queen Suggests:
Take Care

Think about your daily habits. Are they healthy? What improvements might you make in your diet, your exercise program, your work environment, your family life, your friendships, or in other aspects of your routine to improve your well-being?

If you decide to make changes in your life, be realistic in your expectations. Your goal is not to be as you were at thirty, it is to be your best Self today and tomorrow.

Adopt the changes you decide on with your full Intention and Attention. If you want a certain result, you must work to actualize it.

Think about caring for yourself as an act of love, rather than an odious duty. Attitude is all. Your self-care is, after all, strictly a gift you are giving to yourself.

Eat well.

Sleep enough.

Exercise your body and your mind.

Play hard.

Laugh often.

Defend your needs.

Be patient with yourself. Change is slow and you are human.

The physical plane connects us with the here and now—it is the world as we perceive it through our five senses, the life that we embody. Real Life. The most effective way to nurture ourselves, body and soul, is to treat the minutiae of our dailiness, the mundane and the profane parts of our life, in a consciously celebratory manner. When we practice the art of approaching all facets of life with the same dedicated devotion that one would apply to an important ritual occasion, and the craft of making every detail matter and every minute really count, we are validating our own worth and importance. It is this constant presence in the present that ultimately nourishes and energizes us.

I have a simple philosophy. Fill what's empty. Empty what's full. And scratch where it itches.
—Alice Roosevelt Longworth,
American writer (1884-1980)

By middle age, most of us have lost already, or will soon lose, our parents, perhaps even spouses, best friends, and significant others. Who will mother us now? Who will take care of us, or more important maybe, who will care whether we take care of ourselves? Now is the time for us to learn how to be our own caring best friend, sister, daughter, and mother. And this is our chance to be the sort of parent that we always wanted—for me it was the cheerful, optimistic, fun-loving Mary Poppins type that my little girl-Self needed so badly. But whatever our childhood was like, that was then and this is now. Now, we can give ourselves the unconditional love and support that we did or did not have as we were growing up. We can and must assume the responsibility to feed, nurture, encourage, and comfort ourselves, pamper and challenge ourselves, whisper into our own ear each night as we slip off to sleep, "Good night, honey. I love you."

The Queen Suggests:
Feed Yourself

When is the last time someone cooked a special meal for you? When is the last time you cooked a special meal especially for yourself? What are you waiting for? If you are never alone at dinnertime, do lunch. Or brunch or breakfast or high tea or a midnight snack.

Create an out-of-the-ordinary menu that might include your favorite culinary treats, or foods that you have always meant to try. Or you may want to create a fantasy feast or recreate a memorable meal from your childhood, from your travels to exotic places, or from your favorite book.

Cook with the Intention to nourish and please yourself, purposefully infusing the food with love and Attention, just as you would in anticipation of any honored guest.

Set your table with all of the special things that you love, but never use. Enjoy your grandmother's plate or vase, cloth napkins, and your good stemware. Create a centerpiece that honors and celebrates you. Have fresh flowers or foliage or your favorite houseplant. Set out some of your amulets or holy items that represent your Intention to treat your Self well. Light candles to ignite your Intention.

Pour a libation of wine or iced tea and offer a toast to you, your health, your happiness, your life.

Don't forget to say grace. Bless your Self and your bountiful blessings.

Time spent in the bath, with a good book, exercising, and even doing domestic routines, can feel like holy rites of devotion if we perform them with the focused intention of Self-care and concern. Our concentration = consecration. Meals, for instance can certainly be something more than the mere rushed intake of calories, nutrients, television news, and family bickering. A normal supper can be one of life's most agreeable ceremonies if we establish a comfortable, leisurely, aesthetic, emotionally safe environment in which to enjoy food and convivial company even— *especially*—if it is "only" our own.

Bountiful blessings of the elements.
Bountiful blessings of the moment.
Bountiful blessings of the ancestors.
Bountiful blessings of ourselves.
Bountiful blessings of each other.
Bountiful blessings of our association.
Bountiful blessings of our affection.
Bountiful blessings of our experience.
Bountiful blessings of our emotions.
Bountiful blessings of our intentions.
Bountiful blessings of our effort.
Bountiful blessings of our attention.
Bountiful blessings of our action.
Bountiful blessings of our effect.

—D. H.

The Queen deserves the very best.

One thing that was made painfully clear to me during my years in the hospice zone is the importance of using everything that we have—while we can—and the folly of saving favorite items for *something, someday* special. Somehow, the days never seem special enough to allow ourselves the pleasure, the indulgence, to use and enjoy the very things that we love the most. Every day, after all, is just another day, and so we let them pass, and then, one day, we run out of days. Goddess-forbid that we would dare to feel that *we* were special enough.

If we are to treat ourselves like company, we must provide ourselves with the best that we have to offer—our best attitude, our best care, our best possessions. When my mother died, I inherited my grandmother's set of turn-of-the-century hand-painted china. I have always loved those dishes, which evoke fond memories of Gramma's excellent Jewish cooking and her unconditional love. When my grandmother died, my mother took the set home with her, wrapped each piece carefully in tissue paper, and put them all away for use only on special occasions. For a while, while I was growing up, we enjoyed my grandmother's dishes at holiday suppers when they were filled with company-only extravagances like black olives and pickled watermelon rinds.

But as time passed and the family dispersed, special occasions became rare and I didn't see those dishes for years. Now that they are mine, I, too, cherish them and use them only for very special occasions. Every Meal. Every Day. For my Self. I am careful with them, but I use them anyway. If I break one occasionally, I feel bad for a moment, then I put the pieces on the soil of my potted plants where their pattern continues to cheer me. If there are none left by the time I die, so be it. One less find for the Antiques Road Show.

*I would live my life burning it up as I go along,
so that at the end nothing is left unused.*

—May Sarton, American writer and poet (1912-1995)

As we continue to practice living life with Intention, Attention, purpose, and appreciation, we are called to take stock on every level imaginable—material, mental, emotional, and spiritual. Now we take the time to catalogue what it is we have, what we have accumulated, what we hold onto, what we carry with us through the years. And we evaluate everything in terms of its value to us. Do our belongings, attitudes, ideas, obligations, commitments, habits, goals, dreams, relationships, and wardrobes still fit us? Are they flattering? Do they please us? Do they continue to serve us? Do they feed us what we need? Or do they drain our energy and slow us down by the amount of maintenance that they require?

Now that we are about to step up and out into the world as sovereigns, poised to soar, it is time check our baggage and lighten up our load. It seems to me that we spend the first half of our lives accumulating things, and the second half getting rid of them, paring our possessions down to a manageable cache. It is common for women in midlife to display an overwhelming urge to purge, to clean out, throw out, refuse, release, discard, to distill and streamline all of our attachments. We refine our needs and tastes and want to be surrounded by only those people, places, and things that add something positive to our lives. When we clear out the inessentials, we make space for ourselves to grow and expand to fill the void.

An orderly house always seems like the invitation to a fresh start, which is why so many cultures incorporate a thorough house scrubbing, a clean sweep, as it were, as well as an internal ablution in their New Year's rituals. Our messy thinking and sloppy habits come more easily into focus when our surroundings are tidy and beautiful and filled only with what is

The Queen Suggests:
House Cleaning from the Inside Out

Throw out, re-cycle, or donate one thing every day. This is a great practice in claiming what is important to you and discarding what is not.

Spend an evening in the closet playing dress-up. Get rid of everything that doesn't fit your figure or your evolved Self-image.

Eliminate one food from your diet that you know you should not eat. When you get used to living without it, eliminate one more.

Send all of the novels that you know you will never re-read to a school or hospital library. And that pile of magazines, too.

Clean out your paper and computer files, your address book, old correspondence, and tax records. How much of that clutter is really relevant any more?

Do the same with your medicine cabinet and cosmetic drawers. How many of the products crammed in there merely mask superficial symptoms and flaws rather than enhance your essential strength and beauty?

Remove yourself from situations and relationships that no longer nurture you. Refuse what does not interest you.

Monitor your thoughts, and edit the negative, Self-derogatory ones in midstream. Eliminate stinking thinking.

Reduce stress through yoga, exercise, breathing techniques, warm baths, sex, music, art, and meditation.

Eliminate the accumulated toxins in your body by fasting occasionally.

Slough off the old, like a snake shedding its skin, or a butterfly its cocoon. Emerge renewed and energized.

meaningful. With the chaff, the distractions, and cluttered corners of our minds cleared away, we can better see the structure of our lives, the foundations of our support, the bare bones that comprise our true Selves. With practice, we can distinguish which messages come directly from our souls as expressed through our true desires, needs, values, and aesthetics, and which do not. Which relationships serve us in a reciprocal manner and which do not. Which engagements, involvements, and assignments are fulfilling and life-affirming and which are empty busywork. "It's not so much how busy you are, but why you are busy," the writer Marie O'Conner reminds us. "The bee is praised; the mosquito is swatted."

The more conscious and respectful we become of the abiding presence and guiding force of the Queen in our lives, the more we feel inclined to spend time alone in Her excellent company. One way to honor these healing times of communion, of seclusion, and of reflection with that deep part of our Selves that is the source of our strength and wisdom is to conduct them in an environment that is worthy of the occasion. That source, that center of Self, cries out to inhabit a special, sanctified space of our own creation, "a room of one's own" as Virginia Woolf put it, where we are happily at home within ourselves. The Queen becomes very discriminating as to the quality of peace, order, and beauty that She establishes in Her environment, and She defends its inviolability as sacred.

———————

The Queen Suggests:
Create Sacred Space

Put some meditative music on, dim the lights, and walk, dance, slide, crawl, or roll, slowly through your home. You might want to close or squint your eyes so that you can concentrate on what you feel rather than what you see. Do you feel yourself drawn to a particular area or corner? That is your *sitio*, your particular sacred space. This is the place where you can feel most strongly your connections to the energy of the Earth, to spirit, and to your inner best Self.

Your *sitio* can be as large as a room, as small as a chair or rug, as contained and hidden as a closet. It can be a sitting area or desk space in a larger room. It can be under a dormer in the attic, or even outside in the yard or on the porch.

Claim this space as sacred.

Cleanse your *sitio*. Wash the floor, windows, and whatever furniture or shelves are in your space. Burn some incense to smudge away any negative energy. Frankincense, sage, cedar, camphor, and copal are especially effective purifying agents.

Consecrate your *sitio*. Bless your sacred space with the intention that it be a safe and comfortable haven for you, a shelter from the storms of living where you can always find your center and reconnect with your Self.

Sanctify your *sitio* by creating an altar with some amulets or altar items that will continually remind you of the purpose of your Intention. The amount of space and privacy you have will determine the size and form of your altar.

You can construct an actual altar with many holy icons, lucky charms, inspiring images, offerings, and candles. You can discretely place certain personally (and privately) precious items on your desk or dresser top, bookshelf, or windowsill. You can create a drawer or cabinet or closet altar that is completely hidden to all but you.

Claim and defend adequate blocks of time to spend in your sacred space so that you might engage with your Self on a regular basis. Use your sacred time and space to write in your journal, listen to music, meditate, do your yoga or exercises, dance, read, daydream, or nap.

With Self-engagement and development on your mind, any time can be auspicious and any place a sanctuary. All you need do is claim it.

The Queen of Swords chooses Contemplation.
With sharp mind, whittling away confusion,
She fathoms and fashions Her own worth.

Our mental function is not satisfied with simply accessing our Intentions. Our minds want to know what they mean and how they affect us. Our conscious, rational aspect craves order, information, comprehension. We humans seem to have a basic need to organize, classify, and characterize the world around us. When we apply this same need for knowledge and understanding to our inner world—our emotions, thoughts, instincts, and intuitions—we are able to extract their value. What can we learn from what we feel? And how can we use these feelings to our benefit?

By keeping track of the circumstances and situations of our lives and our own conscious and unconscious responses to them, we can plot our course, chart our progress, project our aspirations, alter our habits, adjust our attitudes, and plan our actions. "The decision to write a journal," writes Christine Baldwin in *Life's Companion: Journal Writing as a Spiritual Quest,* "has been the most important decision I have ever made because it has led to every other important decision I've ever made. The existence of the journal provides writers with confidence and courage that we can travel as far as the mind allows, and find our way home through the act of writing".

The blueprints and maps for our lives can be found in the documentation that we keep. When we record our thoughts, feelings, dreams, coincidences, ideas, inspirations, and omens, we have the raw data that we need to figure out what it is that we already know as well as what we still

The Queen Suggests:
Note the Process of Noting Your Process

Keep track of your life and living.

Keep written, recorded, and/or visual journals of collages, drawings, or photographs that record and comment on your:

Dreams	Interactions
Feelings	Memories
Goals	Miracles
Happenings	Omens
Hunches	Physical concerns
Impulses	Plans
Instincts	Thoughts

Keep your inherited and personal herstorical records:

Almanacs	Letters From You
Autograph Books	Letters To You
Calendars	Lists
Date Books	Photographs
Diaries	Scrapbooks
Family Bibles	Year Books

If you do any sort of divinatory readings or consult any oracles, keep notes on these sessions:

Astrology Charts	Palm Readings
Automatic Writings	Psychic Readings
Crystal Ball	Runes
I Ching	Tarot

Put 'em together and what have you got? Bibbidi-Bobbidi-YOU!

need to learn. I call this practice, "Noting the Process of Noting the Process." I use the term "practice" advisedly. Practice implies Attention, concentration, and discipline. But the mental effort and dedication required is well rewarded by the Self-knowledge that we stand to gain.

The word "practice" also serves to remind us that there is no perfect. Whether we maintain a spiritual practice, a creative practice, or a professional practice, we are always in the process of learning, adapting, accommodating, growing, and changing. The end only comes when we die. In the meantime, all we have is the means, the very process of living itself. We try, we move forward, we trip, we fall behind, we start again, and eventually we become, while not perfect, perfectly wonderful Queens.

Our dreams are one of the most accessible avenues to our inner Selves, so it is very important to capture them and try to decipher their meaning. There, in the nocturnal operatic extravaganzas created by our sleeping mind, we live a sort of mirror image, inside-out version of our waking lives, filled with puns, coded messages, quirky clues, malaprops, and clever metaphors. In our dreamtime, we revisit the past, rehashing, reshaping, rethinking old scenarios and their ultimate ramifications. We experience the present in sharper Technicolor focus, garnering deeper, more profound layers of perception. And we envision the future, writing a variety of potential story lines and trying them on for size. "Without leaps of imagination or dreaming, we lose the excitement of possibilities," writes Gloria Steinem. Really, we dream up our lives.

Getting in touch with the truth of our dreams and feelings means that we have the wherewithal to monitor and evaluate all the subtle frequencies that transmit vital information to us, as well as our visceral reactions to them. An impulse is just that. An electrical buzz that we actually, albeit subliminally, *feel*. We have all had the experience of walking on the beach and being moved to pick up a shell or a pebble. Why did we choose that particular one and not the all but identical one next to it? Because this one called our name. "Pssst. Over here. Pick me." And we heard it. Well, I

The Queen Suggests:
Keep a Dream Book

When we record our dreams, we stimulate our memory of them, acknowedge their value, and invite further dreams in the future.

Buy or make a beautiful notebook. It should be something really special, for it is to be the repository of your precious dreams.

Before going to bed, take a relaxing hot bath. This will loosen your muscles, reduce your stress and your resistance, and open your pores, as it were, to receive the messages from your unconscious mind.

Set your Intention to dream and to remember your dreams.

Place your dream book in a convenient place near your bed so that you can just roll over and write before you are completely awake. When you transcribe your dream in this semi-sleep state, your conscious mind will not so easily interfere with your unconscious.

Or, if you are a Queen like me and only wake up when you have to pee, keep your dream book and pen near the toilet. It is an extraordinarily liberating experience to let your waters and your stream of consciousness flow together!

Date each entry and inscribe any other relevant information, such as where you were when you had the dream if you were not at home, whether you were menstruating or fasting, or if the moon was new or full. This will become more meaningful over time and you will be glad of these additional clues.

Draw your dreams. This can take the form of an actual illustration of the content, or a free-flowing sketch of the feeling of it.

Draw upon the imagery in your dreams and the information and understanding gleaned from them to solve problems and create innovative solutions in your work, social interactions, and personal growth.

Save these records of all your dreams and spend time with them once in a while. With each reading they will acquire another layer of relevance for you. When you read your entire dream collection, you will notice recurring themes, repeated symbols, familiar locations and characters, and you will see the logic of your word play and visual patterns. You will become proficient in the symbolic language spoken by your Self.

always say, "If the phone rings, answer it." If it occurs to you—if you think it, dream it, feel it, sense it, intuit it—it's yours. We just need the confidence and courage to recognize and own the knowledge offered by this great airy resource.

With time, we come to honor and depend upon the veracity of our inner thoughts and feelings to offer direction and meaning to our lives. When we begin to pay serious, disciplined Attention to the inner process of our journey, we start to notice the serendipity, coincidence, and synchronicity that surround us. We become more sensitive to the special, uncanny, lucky surprises that keep popping up in our path. Soon we begin to recognize these personally relevant occurrences as omens, and it behooves us to take very careful note of them. They are the guideposts of our soul's journey toward itself, the psychic maps that help to show us the way to go and keep us on the right track.

Like divine affirmations, these meaningful signs and signals serve to assure us that we are in the right place at the right time. They are road markers inscribed in our own private language, leading us along the long Queen's Highway. Some people find money wherever they go. Others could walk with their heads down, eyes perpetually scanning, waving around a metal detector, and never find a single penny. Some people find shells or feathers or spiders or sea glass or rainbows or certain number combinations. Each of these items represents something particular to the people who recognize them. My friend Dominique finds heart-shaped stones. To her, they symbolize the mission of the "heartist," which is her life's chosen work. Each rock she encounters is like a small pat on the back. My dear friend Kay finds doll arms. Doll arms! They remind her of the little metal Mexican charms called *milagros* (miracles) that she loves. Whenever I come across a heart stone or doll arm, I know that our paths have crossed that day.

Impulses, instinct, intuitions, feelings, and dreams are like any other skill. They need to be respected, maintained, used, and cherished. My own

The Queen Suggests:
Map Reading Lessons

What colors, numbers, objects hold special meaning for you whenever you come across them? Have you had this sense of connection since childhood or is it recent?

What do these clues mean to you and why? Perhaps they recall a fond memory, a symbolic association, or a fortunate magical significance.

Notice how and when these signs and symbols present themselves to you. Notice how they make you feel. What is the question that they answer?

Make a mental note or journal entry of the occurrence of the omen and its meaning for you. Make special notation of your appreciation of this sign, this clue, this nod of approval.

Keep your eyes and ears open. If you keep looking for omens, directions, connections, synchronicities, messages, and miracles, you will certainly find them everywhere.

So, then, what is the difference between a seeker and a seer?

life is littered with signs and portents, and of course I pick them all up, as unsanitary as that might seem. Once in a while I don't bend down to gather something up. I am too lazy perhaps, or distracted, or in a rush. But when this happens, I always force myself to return to the site, even if it's blocks away, because when we disregard our omens, we lose the ability to recognize them. How many times have we left the house without an umbrella despite our "flash" that it was going to rain? And doesn't it always? When we ignore our inner voice, we stop hearing what we are trying to tell ourselves, causing our internal instinctual compass to malfunction, leaving us on the long and winding road without any breadcrumbs to follow.

A well-developed, active interior life provides us with direction and strength for the journey. When we grow and the situations of our lives start to flow, when the going is good and the living gets easier, it seems only natural to be thankful. But what about all those times when nothing seems to budge? When we are stuck in the rush hour traffic jam of daily life and our bodies and souls start to feel like banged up bumper cars? When we are tested and pounded and pummeled? When things seem so crazy we wonder what do we have to be thankful for?

The greatest gift of the mind is, perhaps, perspective. Our reflective, rational side keeps us in balance, helps us from running away with our emotions. "Well," my best friend Daile once calmly commented in the midst of an intense work disaster that would normally have driven her quite mad, "at least nobody died." That's it, exactly. If we have a healthy sense of perspective, our lives become infinitely more precious to us and we automatically operate with an attitude of gratitude. People who have themselves been ill or who care-take others have earned a certain understanding of this point of view. Aging helps, too. Even so, for most of us it is a daily, hourly, minutely learned lesson—one that we easily forget. One that we would be wise to remember.

———

The Queen Suggests:
A Moving Meditation of Appreciation

Take a walk someplace nice. Alone.
With each step you take, name one good thing that you have in your life.
Something for which you are thankful. Recite this aloud or silently.

Step. My health.
Step. My friends.
Step. My job.
Step. My dog.
Step. A new friend.
Step. A secure home.
Step. The clouds.
Step. The beautiful moon.
Step. That certain memory.
Step. Not knowing war.
Step. Two feet.

The list is endless, gratitude boundless.

Thank Goodness!

*The Queen of Cups chooses Seclusion.
There She sits in the shadows of Her
own depth and dares to feel Her feelings.*

Certainly the most crucial step toward sovereignty is to know our Selves. After all our years as mothers and others, we need to reestablish who we are as individuals, separate and distinct from our relationships with those around us. Who am I if I am not a mother, a daughter, a lover, a wife, a friend, a partner, a teacher, a student, a boss, or an employee? Who am I if I am not associated with some undertaking, enterprise, creation, project, product, or service? Who am I, in fact, if I just am? As I live and breathe? And how do I feel about it? For these answers and the answers to all of life's questions, we must look into our hearts and allow ourselves to feel our feelings, to own and embrace them for the wisdom they convey. Marion Woodman, the Jungian analyst, writer, and specialist in female development, calls this process, "coming home to ourselves."

Soul searching, like the practice of any devotion, requires solitude, quiet, and quality time. But life is hectic and our inner needs have long been relegated to the bottom of our endless to-do lists, our dreams and desires deferred, left on the back burner to simmer. Over a hundred years ago, Florence Nightingale observed, "Women never have a half-hour in all their lives (excepting before or after anybody is up in the house) that they can call their own, without fear of offending or of hurting someone. Why do people sit up so late, or, more rarely, get up so early? Not because the day is not long enough, but because they have no time in the day to them-

The Queen Suggests:
A Mirror Meditation

An excellent way to start to know your Self is by taking a good long look at yourself in the mirror. This seemingly simple practice is not so easy, as most of us are mirror-shy, accustomed as we are to using mirrors as weapons of Self-destruction.

Sit comfortably and look into a mirror. Resist the urge to check your hair for neatness or your teeth for spinach. Under no circumstance allow your mind to travel toward judgment or critique. And be nice. Spare yourself those nasty little mind-jabs of disappointment and disapproval.

Look at yourself as you would a stranger, with an open mind and an open heart. Do not avert your eyes, but employ them in a straightforward, fearless manner. Introduce yourself to the woman you see there. Let your eyes reassure her that you are friendly.

Gaze into her eyes to try to grasp the sense of who she might be. Relax into that gaze and stay engaged for as long as you can. Peer into the depths of your being. What do you see there? What memories? What motives? What myths? What messages?

If the eyes are, indeed, the mirrors of our soul, we have much to learn by looking deeply into them. It's like sending a bucket into a deep well and drawing up the clear, revitalizing waters of wisdom from the source.

selves." If our Intention is to know ourselves and to grow our power, we require dependable periods of uninterrupted time and inviolate space that we can call our own, a protected seclusion conducive to our sacred Self-communion.

Whether we are married, dating, divorced, or single, it is crucial that we learn how to cherish being alone without being lonely. Solitude is a gift of love that we give to ourselves. If we can manage to enjoy our own company, to entertain and please ourselves, we will not feel dependent upon someone else to make us happy. If we can soothe and support ourselves, offer ourselves understanding and insights, we release ourselves from the need for outside affirmation. Knowing that we don't *need* someone else to complete and fulfill our lives affords us a new confidence in our own ability to cope and flourish. This, in turn, relieves us and our present and future partners of a great deal of pressure, as it allows us to participate in our familial and friendly relationships on more equal footing, with fewer unrealistic expectations and cause for recriminations.

Seclusion is withdrawal on all levels. It means separating our identity not only from other people, but also from outwardly dictated and directed activity as well. Sometimes it is necessary to step back a few paces from our bustling lives, to stop racing around, and just slow down so that we can absorb and process our experiences. In a culture that defines itself in terms of clocks and dollars and duty, it is difficult to allow ourselves to claim the time and mental space to devote to an occupation that results in no visible product. Non-product, however, and nonproductive are definitely not the same thing. Down time is not negative. It is *not* not doing something. What we are doing when we jump off of the treadmill is resting, reflecting, ruminating, regenerating, rejoicing, and opening to the myriad ways of receiving the reassurance and guidance that we need.

When we carve out a niche in our busy lives to do the sorts of things that feed our soul, we are affirming our Self-worth, acknowledging that we crave and deserve our own undivided Attention. When we claim

The Queen Suggests:
A Day in Bed

For years, I have been practicing a Ceremony of Seclusion for myself that I call my Day in Bed Ritual. There will simply come a day—I can never predict which day—when I wake up knowing that today is my Day in Bed. I know with a deep knowing that if I don't lie down, I will fall down, collapse under the strain. I do not feel sick, mind you, just out of steam. In my mind, this is not a sick day, but rather, a Well Day, a day to devote to my own inner needs. Over time, I have learned not to fight this overwhelming laziness. I gladly give in and let go of my goals.

I get up long enough to make a cup of tea and bring it back to bed with me, where I stay for the next 24 hours. Oh, I get up periodically to pee- and drink and muster up something to eat, but after each brief foray, I return to bed to spend the day blissfully quiet and alone. I read. I nap. I spend time with my journal, write a letter or a list or two. I masturbate. I read. I nap. I luxuriate in doing nothing. I imagine myself to be Elizabeth Barrett Browning or Colette or some other fabulously romantic invalid writer propped up on a throne of pillows, her devoted dog or cat nestled in the covers at her feet.

These short periods of respite and regeneration work remarkably well to keep me cool, centered, and balanced. And best of all, I rarely get sick.

the psychic space and set aside the personal time to pursue the knowledge and mastery of our Selves—when we assume the entitlement, the ability, and the authority to do so—we are able to access and transform our perceptions, our perspectives, our experience, our expectations, and, in the process, our entire reality. By taking the time, by taking our time, we bless ourselves with true devotion. We consecrate our precious lives, and celebrate the continuously wondrous miracle of the unfolding of our Selves.

These exercises in Self-appreciation and affection are not meant to seal ourselves off from others forever, or to replace any current or future relationships, but to make sure that we do not get involved for the wrong reasons—out of fear or desperation. We emerge from these exercises with the secure knowledge that we are our own best lover. And when and if we choose, we are able to share that love with someone special who will understand how precious it is and return it in kind.

Sacred Seclusion enables us to know, own, and honor ourselves as unique, individual entities. To admit our abilities and limitations, our talents and truculence on the physical, mental, emotional, and spiritual planes, and to love ourselves with compassion and no judgement attached. A practice of solitude and separation—be it occasional, frequent, or constant—teaches us that we do not need the approval or permission of any outside source to validate our personal experience or emotions. In knowing who we are, we are empowering ourselves to know what we know and feel what we feel.

We can only discover our own truth by paying close Attention to the promptings of our inner Selves and to our honest reactions to the external energies that surround us. But just because we have the ability to access our emotional and intuitive truths doesn't mean that we necessarily want to. In fact, most of us have a huge resistance to facing our emotions and letting ourselves simply feel. This is especially true when we are confronted with the adversity, fear, and loss that comes with the hard times in life. Who wants to feel like that? We bemoan our fate, our bad luck, our sad fortune, and find it easier to feel sorry for ourselves than to actually *experience*

The Queen Suggests:
A Love Affair with Your Self

Get to know your Self. Acknowledge your thoughts and feelings, your fears and fantasies. Spend some quality time alone together—just you, yourself, and you. Turn off the computer, the phone, the fax, and the TV. Put on your favorite music, or simply savor the silence. Entertain a program of non-directed Self-discovery. Stare out the window or into a candle flame or a mirror. Clear your mind of inner chatter and let it wander where it will.

Take an interest in your Self. Engage in projects of Self-expression in order to reconnect with your higher nature and your inner best Self. Do an exercise tape. Go for a run, walk, swim, or bike ride. Read your Tarot cards. Consult the *I Ching*. Do yoga. Meditate. Drum, chant, dance. Write in your journal. Transcribe your dreams. Create an altar. Paint a picture or your walls. Sing silly songs. Have a good cry. Pound on pillows and scream. Laugh out loud.

Please your Self. Work at establishing a warm, rich atmosphere for your own physical comfort and aesthetic enjoyment. Indulge in a variety of sensory delights. Surround yourself—your body, your home, and to whatever degree possible, your office—with the colors, textures, sounds, and smells that you love and that express your personality. Light candles and incense.

Court your Self. Get all dressed up purely for the fun of it. Take yourself on a dream date. Go somewhere you have been meaning to go. Do things that you love. Buy yourself special treats. Compliment yourself, applaud and appreciate your strength and your beauty. Whisper sweet somethings in your ear. Tickle your fancy. Pull down the shades, turn off the lights, and dance till you drop. Massage your body with sweet oils. Kiss yourself. Masturbate. Make yourself a marvelous breakfast in the morning. Send yourself flowers with a note saying, "I love you."

the pain when we are stricken with sorrow or sadness. We are exposed and vulnerable, scared silly, like a child who needs a nightlight, forgetting that the light is already on inside. We panic, preferring anything to the deep pitch, the petrifying recesses, of our own souls. This terror is the turning point, the time for determination.

It is at this critical moment, that we can consciously choose to dwell in the dark for a spell—for as long as it takes—*despite* our resistance and fear. We can decide to confront the emotions that churn beneath our surface. We can choose to engage with them, to follow them wherever they take us. To explore the blind byways of our pain, inching along, feeling our way through the tunnels with our tongues if we have to. To plumb our emotional depths and mine that precious secret ore of our own poignant life experience. To feel our hearts actually break, explode apart like a geode, revealing the glittering crystals of our wisdom growing inside. Once we have connected with our emotions, identified them, listened to their stories, felt their unutterable pain, confusion, grief, and joy, we can accept them as our teachers, bow to their great lessons, embrace them with love, and then release them into the night.

If we don't locate our feelings, you better believe they will come looking for us. We try to turn off what we don't want to deal with—the constant bombardment of cynicism, negativity, and violence in the outer world and the steady accumulation of stress in our daily lives. Often, we aren't even consciously aware that we are annoyed, upset, depressed, dispirited. We simply carry on. We persevere. We do what we need to do. We conscientiously continue on continuing on, ignoring our feelings, suppressing our sadness. Until the day comes when we can stand it no longer. What we need then is a good cry. But, then again, when we are numb with denial, we can't always cry. We want to. We need to. But we can't let go. We are bound tight by some excruciating kind of crippling constipation of expression.

The Queen Suggests:
A Ceremony for Dampened Spirits

Set aside a weekend when you can be alone.

Rent at least twelve tearjerker tapes or DVDs.

Stock up on your favorite comfort foods, if you wish. I usually do this ceremony while fasting, but you can treat yourself with ice cream or wine or Chinese food or whatever else you crave for indulgent solace.

Take a long, hot bath to wash away any resistance and to completely open your pores and your heart.

Settle into bed or onto the sofa for the marathon. Make sure you have handy a box of ultra soft tissues, or better yet, a pile of lace trimmed, embroidered, and crocheted hankies.

Turn on the TV and let it flow, let it flow, let it flow.

Recently, I experienced a series of disappointments and setbacks. I stewed and stomped and swore, but I couldn't find acceptance and release. Then, one evening after bending down to put something away, I stood up quickly and smacked my head into an open kitchen cabinet door. That did it. I burst into tears, bawled like a baby, and within moments I felt much, much better. There is nothing quite so satisfying as a really cathartic cry. Tears are cleansing and refreshing, but there are certainly more agreeable ways to achieve the unburdening relief that they offer than by banging your head against a wall. Over the years, I have developed a personal ritual, a Cryfest, where I shamelessly indulge myself in the consolation of blatant lamentation. For two solid days I allow myself to weep and wallow, really revel in royal melancholy, after which I am renewed and ready to face anything once again.

Madonna Virgo Dolorosa

Queen of Love and Pain and Sadness,
Long-Suffering Lady of Perpetual Sorrows,
Purified by Her tears.
Who pursues the path of heartfelt passion
To heights and depths and breadths unfathomed.
Who practices faith and patience; infinite persistence,
Trusting, come what may.
Who plunges directly through the darkness,
Through the swamps and sweats, the sucking shallows,
Through twisted tunnels and around blind bends,
Through delusion, through denial,
Through to destined ends.

—D. H.

The Queen Suggests:
Light Your Fire

According to the Chinese spatial wisdom of Feng Shui, your stove represents the heat, the hearth-energy, the central furnace of your home and your Self as well.

If you, like most of us, customarily use only one or two burners for most of your cooking, you are symbolically limiting your power potential.

To symbolize the strength of your inner fire, light all four burners once a day, even for just a moment, to activate and intensify your potency and to remind yourself to utilize the full heat of your resources.

Remember this fiery image when you want to be "cooking on all four burners," as the saying goes.

The Queen of Wands chooses Creation.
She lights the spark, the flame, ignites
the courage, to claim Her potent force.

So it all comes to this. All of the accumulated experience and growth over the course of our lifetime, all of the hard work of our midlife transition, all of our concentrated efforts to become who it is we truly are, all of our conscientious development on the physical, mental, and emotional planes, are brought together now in the spiritual realm. For it is here that we find the inspiration, the will, the determination, and the courage to claim, proclaim, demand, and command our lives as our own. Our purest Intentions and our deepest Attention; our dedicated attitudes of Self-Defense, Self-Discipline, Self-Devotion, and Self-Determination; and our willingness to explore Consolation. Reflection, and Seclusion have combined to lead us to this point of no return. All that is left now to do is to add that energetic charge, that fiery force that is required to actualize it all. We are all but ready and set to go on our way, out into the world as righteous and powerful women, rulers of the lives that we choose. We are like firecrackers on the 3rd of July. Above all, we must grant ourselves the permission to think big and expect the best, to imagine the full range of life's energizing possibilities, and to allow ourselves to experience our own infinite capacity for growth, transformation, renewal, and joy.

Where do we find this energizing fire spirit? How can we access its potent energy of inspiration and will so that we can ignite our reality and boost our determination to create it? And how can we harness it to fuel our

The Queen Suggests:
Breathe Fire

Tap into your own source of primal energy.

This *Kundalini* breathing technique called the "Breath of Fire" is used to activate the solar plexus, or the third chakra, which is the center associated with fire, power, and strength. A rapid, rhythmic, continuous breath, it also helps to fire and charge your internal systems and raise your level of Chi. Eventually, it allows you to stand solid in your pervasive inner truth of "I Am."

To begin, take a deep breath in and feel your stomach relaxing outward. Exhale. Inhale again. As you exhale this time, pull your solar plexus back toward the spine with a pumping action. (Your solar plexus is just above your navel.) Your exhalation should sound like a sniff. Immediately relax your solar plexus and let the air rush back in with a sniff.

Now, without any pause between breaths in and out, continue this pumping action with sniffs at each inhalation and exhalation.

Your chest should be slightly lifted. All your breathing should be done through the nose and with both nostrils at once.

Your lungs are never completely full or empty during the Breath of Fire. Rather, air is vibrated in and out of them through the plunging movements of the diaphram.

Your power center is now working like a bellows to bring the belly fire of your center up to the surface where you can feel and make use of it. The entire potential of the universe flows in and out of you in endless circulation.

Your breath feeds the flames and the flames feed you.

aspirations? This creative, enabling, vivifying power of the universe has been called by many names. It is known in Chinese and other Far Eastern cultures as Chi and in Hindu tradition as *Kundalini*, "the sacred energy that awakens consciousness." In the West, the psychologist Carl Jung called it Anima—the fundamental, primal, unifying power of movement, growth, change, and transformation that is the life force itself. This ultimate energetic wisdom exists all around us on every level. It surges like an electric pulse through the vast cosmos, through the Earth, and through all the life forms that dwell here. It is deep within each one of us, as well, waiting to be summoned, called up, employed.

> *And I am the Queen of Wands*
> *Who burns, who glows, who webs*
> *The message strands,*
> *Who stands, who always will.*
> *—Judy Grahn, American poet (1940-)*

The vast pools of our creative resources are contained in the *chakras* in our bodies. *Chakra* is a Sanskrit word meaning "wheel, or vortex," and it refers to each of the seven energy centers of which our consciousness, our energy system, is composed. In midlife, the *Kundalini* energy that has been coiled like a dormant snake at the base of our spine begins to rise, bringing with it the energy from the bottom of our torso up through all of our *chakras*, charging each one as it goes. All of the energy that once was concentrated in our sexual and productive centers now strives to rise like a cobra ascending from its containing basket. Ultimately, it emerges through the crown *chakra* at the top of our heads, up and out to join our power, and our awareness of our power, with that of the entire universe.

Both of the words "inspiration" and "aspiration" come from the same Latin root that means "to breathe." They are both related to the Latin

The Queen Suggests:
Eat Fire

In addition to being loaded with vitamin C and being excellent for colds, cayenne pepper is a great blood and liver cleanser, an endorphin enhancer, and even a foot warmer. It also helps you to dislodge blocked energy that prevents you from speaking your truth.

Place some cayenne on the tip your tongue. If you do not like hot sensations, put it way in the back of the tongue where there are fewer taste buds.

After your tongue stops burning, you will notice the heat seeping into your throat and opening it a little more with each swallow. You can almost picture your throat chakra opening, as if it were a flower bud filmed in slow motion.

You can think of cayenne as powdered courage. Taking cayenne in a ritual context symbolizes fire eating. It enflames our passion to create our reality, and releases the full force of our inner truth, beauty, and wisdom.

word for "spirit." "Inspire" means "to breathe in, to inhale." That is, to take in the spirit, to draw in the power and wisdom of all that is. "Aspire" means "to breathe into or blow upon." It is as simple as that. All we need to do to tune into and benefit from the universal life force is to breathe. Breathing our particular life spirit into all that is. Living a conscious life means to breathe with Intention, to pay Attention to each breath, each moment, rather than coast on automatic pilot. With each inhalation, we can breathe in the wisdom, beauty, and order of the universe, and with each exhalation, we can release our own special and unique creative spirit into the world. As we live and breathe.

If, however, this power encounters a blockage in one of our energy centers as it travels through our body, it gets trapped, hurling and swirling about with nowhere to go. In this case, it causes disturbing symptoms such as menstrual pain, bloating, indigestion, heart palpitations, thyroid problems, headaches, insomnia, and memory loss. Sound familiar? There are many fascinating correspondences between the manifestations of a spiritual awakening of our *Kundalini* energy, which usually occurs in our forties, and the symptoms of menopause. Several wonderful women, such as therapist and energy healer Barbara Brennan, physician Dr. Christiane Northrup, and herbalist Susun Weed, have written extensively about the menopause-*Kundalini* connection. It is very healing to think of hot flashes as power surges that connect us in a new energetic way to the spiritual realms of existence, plugging us directly into the sacred spark of life.

We women of a certain age have gotten pretty familiar with the fiery element. Our bodies are burning up much of the time and so are our tempers. While middle age might be the flash point igniting our spiritual consciousness, it also seems to spark agitation, aggravation, and anger. For many of us, it isn't a question of how to feel the fire within us as much as how to quell it when it becomes unmanageable. Sometimes there is just too much fire. But if we can add a spiritual dimension to our midlife changes and travails on the physical, mental, and emotional planes, we will be able

The Queen Suggests:
A White Bath

Too hot to handle? Feeling burnt out? Nerves, hormones, patience on fire?

Here's a wonderfully calming, cooling bath, great for whenever you are feeling hot and bothered. It is equally refreshing whether you are suffering the hot flash power surges of midlife, the intense heat stress of a city summer, or a simmering anger seething from within.

To be taken three nights in a row, ideally with the light of the moon streaming through your window. Candlelight is lovely as well.

Add to your bath water:
A bouquet of white flowers—lilies, tulips, daisies, roses—whatever most appeals to you.
Some milk. (Think Cleopatra.)
A pinch of white sugar to sweeten.
Perfume or scented oils. (Might I suggest vanilla?)

Steep to the strains of cool jazz, Zen flutes, bird songs, complete silence, or whatever else soothes your soul.

Emerge feeling—and smelling—like dessert. Like some smoothly succulent blanc mange, quivering oh so slightly on the platter.

to experience these changes with an enhanced understanding—even an appreciation—of their ultimate meaning, and we can take steps to ease and support our transitional symptoms. We can let loose this fire power as impatience, sarcasm, disgust, or rage, or we can choose to soothe it, to make it soft and malleable, so that we can mold it to our own specifications and needs.

While menopausal fire, if not well channeled, can certainly scorch us, not to mention those around us, it can also fuel our purpose, our will, and our passion. Fire represents faith, adventure, determination, creativity, curiosity, outreach, and active pursuit. If we learn to let that hot, vibrant breath of life pass freely through us, we can transform it into a kind of metaphoric spark plug that gets our motors running. If we misfire, we become stuck. Ironically, many women in menopause begin to experience some sort of thyroid disorder, a symptom that our fiery energy has become lodged, literally stuck in our throats. The throat chakra is the seat of the Self, the home base of our creativity, our image, our voice, our truth. From here, we project who it is we are into the world. When our energy is blocked, we swallow our power and are prevented from expressing our authentic Selves.

> *What are the words you do not yet have?*
> *What do you need to say? . . . for it is not*
> *difference which immobilizes us, but silence.*
> *And there are so many silences to be broken.*
> —*Audre Lorde, American poet (1934-1992)*

The goal of our spiritual expansion, as always with Queenly pursuits, is to clear our blockages and resistance, and to open ourselves fully to the process of change, engaging ourselves on all levels so that we might grow from the experience. Creation is the alchemical process of burning away the old and useless and recombining the rest into a new synthesized form. However, unblocking our long-held Self-defeating programming and lowering our defenses leaves us vulnerable. It takes an enormous amount of courage to begin. We must be brave enough to open our Selves so that the cosmic blast can shoot through us, inspiring and empowering our hearts, minds, and spirits. This sort of bravery is not blind, however, but more like faith, because it is based on our understanding and absolute trust that change and growth is only possible when we invite and embrace it. Thus does our Queenly transformation become a Self-fulfilling prophecy.

So here we are, finally, at long last, standing at the edge of the promontory of our greatest creation—our own sovereignty. Dare we leap?

When I come to the edge of all the light I know, and am about to step off into the darkness of the unknown, faith is knowing one of two things will happen: either there will be something solid to stand on or I will be taught how to fly.

—Barbara J. Winter, American writer (1942-)

CHAPTER 6

Crowning Glory

CELEBRATING OUR SOVEREIGNTY

Women, please let your own sun, your concentrated energy,
your own submerged authentic vital power shine out from you.
We are no longer the moon. Today we are truly the sun.
We will build shining golden cathedrals at the top of
crystal mountains East of the Land of the Rising Sun.
Women, when you paint your own portrait, do not forget
to put the golden dome at the top of your head.

—*Raicho Hiratsuka, Japanese feminist and publisher (1886-1971)*

*I*n the unforgettable last scene of director Shekhar Kapur's film,
Elizabeth, Elizabeth Tudor is shown preparing to ascend to a troubled
throne. As she engages in an elaborate toilette—a sacred personal ceremony before her public coronation—she symbolically divests herself of all
physical remnants of her early life as a Maiden and washes herself spiritually clean. She cuts off her girlish tresses and dresses her remaining hair,
helmet-like, in rows of tight-to-the-head spiral curls reminiscent of the
hive-crowned Bee Goddess of Neolithic Europe. She discards her pastels
and chiffons and dons a majestic garment with girth and weight. Finally,
she covers her face in a thick layer of impenetrable white paste, a blank
slate, a power mask. In the process of getting dressed she becomes her Self,
Elizabeth the First. Transformed and protected, she steps into her destiny:
The Virgin Queen, beholden to none.

The Queen Suggests:
Crown Your Glory

Create your own majestic makeover. Think about your image. What do you want to project? Do you?

Is your hair your crowning glory? Does it reflect the radiant Queenly you? Or does it just sort of grow out of your head and hang there?

Make a change.

Do something drastic or dramatic or do something simple. It doesn't matter what you do, but do it on purpose. The Queen does nothing by default.

Cut it. Let it grow. Shave it off. Henna it. Style it. Pull it back. Perm it. Braid it. Try bangs. Streak it. Let your natural silver shine through.

Become a blue-haired lady. Or a pink or purple-haired one.

What woman doesn't easily identify with the powerful metaphor of changing her hair, her wardrobe, or her general countenance at critical junctures in her life? The external change can celebrate and illustrate an alteration of attitude or circumstance that we have completed, a transformation from the inside out. Or we can also effect a change as a reminder or incentive to goose along a desired transformation that we are trying to achieve, a change from the outside in.

ASCENDING THE THRONE

While changing our hairstyle, our image, our demeanor, might seem superficial, it can represent symbolically the full range of change— physical, mental, emotional, and spiritual—that we are experiencing, changes that mark our entry into a new phase of our lives. In some traditions, the Crone stage of the Triple Goddess is thought to begin at menopause, while in others, it is said to commence at around fifty-six years of age with a woman's "second Saturn return." This is a reference to Saturn, the teaching planet, which makes its complete twenty-eight-year cycle for a second time at this point in our lives and returns to the exact place in our astrology chart where it appeared at our birth.

To mark these milestones, Croning Ceremonies have become a popular way for women to celebrate a fiftieth birthday. And I, you'll recall, had also long planned to mark the impressive milestone of my fiftieth birthday with a special Croning Ceremony, until I began to think better of it. I definitely did not yet identify myself as a Crone while I was so relatively young, and I was more than half a decade away from my Saturn return. Linking all major midlife transformation to the simple circumstance of turning fifty and marking it with a one-size-fits-all-rite-of-passage struck me as rather arbitrary. A much better idea, it seemed, would be to consider a series of ceremonies to mark all of the various auspicious stages of our ongoing, meandering midlife transitions. One to count our fifth decade, one to mark the cessation of our menses, one to note our Saturn return, and one to celebrate the culmination and resolution of our midlife struggles and our ultimate arrival at the gateway of our personal power.

My own forty-ninth birthday was pivotal. My mother had just died, the last in a long line of loved ones whose passing I had witnessed, and I had just returned home, relieved of my final hospice duties. And, coincidentally, having been born on my mother's birthday, it was the first birthday that I ever had all to myself. It was on that auspicious day that I consciously decided to dedicate myself to the task of healing my past and preparing myself for the regal future that I could just barely begin to envision.

In a sweet, scary, solo ceremony of healthy Self-regard. I lit a candle and declared myself, from that day forth, a divine and beautiful being, a willing participant and eager student open to all of the lessons of life and most worthy of my own love and respect. Instead of fêting myself with cake and ice cream, I fasted, put on some music to meditate by, and composed an affirmation to inspire me through the rest of my change. I laid claim to the vast potential of my ever-increasing powers, and committed myself henceforth to the mastery and management of my Self. But, really, that was just the beginning, the jumping off point for the last lap of my personal marathon toward majesty. I still had a way to go before the fully realized Queen of my Self finally emerged from the *sturm und drang* of my midlife mini-series.

The Queen can show Herself at any time. She moves, unhurried, at Her own pace. She is not bound by age or by blood. Though the process of menopause helps to stimulate the rise of our Kundalini energy, many women stop bleeding and never become Queens. For others, turning fifty is the beginning, not the culmination, of their personal journey into sovereignty. And there are others still, who have perhaps been working steadily toward their own ascendancy for years, who are ready to rise to their highest frequency and proclaim their power when they are much younger. As Billie Burke, who played the good witch in *The Wizard of Oz*, once remarked, "Age is only important if you are a cheese." When we are ready to be Queens, we know it.

Affirmation for My New Self

I am a divine and beautiful being.

I choose to live each moment with appreciation and
   complete acceptance of my own divinity and beauty.

I choose to appreciate and accept the beauty in all
   beings, and the perfect divinity in each moment.

I open my heart to the possibility of love and benefit
   from every being and each moment.

I purge myself of all doubt, negativity, judgmental
   tendencies, guilt, panic, and fearful thinking.

I always seek that which I need to grow, to bud,
   to bloom, to blossom, to fruit, to bear seed.

I dare to draw into myself the positive manifestation
   of each trial and difficulty, the rightness of every lesson.

I breathe deeply and savor the love and benefit that
   surrounds and embraces my life as I live it each moment.

I forgive myself with each breath I take and renew
   my tranceformative intentions with every beat of my heart.

I glory in the goodness and rightness of all that I
   encounter and all that I am.

I am a divine and beautiful being.

   —D. H.

As I began to understand more fully what it means to become a Queen, it occurred to me that what was wanted to mark Her arrival was not a Croning, but a coronation. This realization came to me in an incredibly vivid, compelling, and recurring dream. Even while I slept, my con-

The Queen Suggests:
A True New Decade Celebration

Your forty-ninth birthday is actually much more significant than your fiftieth, because it marks the actual end of the fourth decade of your life and the beginning of the fifth. Technically, a birthday is an anniversary marking the end of a year completed. So, by the time your fiftieth birthday arrives, you have already been fifty years old for a year.

Your forty-ninth birthday is also significant biologically. Our bodies slough off and create new cells all of the time, and it takes a period of seven years to replace them all. Thus, on a cellular level at least, we inhabit a completely and wholly different body every seven years. Forty-nine equals seven times seven, and the start of your eighth round of growth and transformation.

Your forty-ninth birthday is, therefore, the perfect time to consecrate the beginning of this next stage in your life. It might not coincide precisely with your coming into your full power, but you can dedicate yourself to the proposition that you will.

scious Self was completely aware of all of the levels of meaning imbedded in the marvelous metaphorical word play on the theme of "crowning" that my subconscious Self had offered in my sleep: "crowning" as a ritual of royal ordination, "crowning" as the moment when the crown of a baby's head first emerges from the birth canal into a brand new life, "crowning" as the spark of *Kundalini* energy climbing up the spine to be released through the crown *chakra* on top of the head.

There is a wonderful concept in Yoruban culture, the source of the spiritual traditions practiced throughout the African diaspora, that "you crown your own head." That is, we must each take control and make our own lives happen. Even though we are informed, inspired, supported, and strengthened by our roots, our ancestors, and our community, nevertheless, we must ultimately stand alone, Self-authorized and responsible. Thus, a Queen is born.

CROWNING GLORY

Once we know ourselves to be Queens, all that is left now is the blessing. And that, of course, needs to come from within. After all of the introspection and work that we have accomplished as we labored to heal and develop and change and grow, this is the time to own, affirm, and appreciate our best Intentions and efforts. To honor our experience, our hard-won wisdom, our expanded world vision, we bless our path, where we came from, who we are, and who we are becoming. Now that we are focused and clear, we can embrace our Selves with the same compassionate care that we offer to others so freely, accepting our weakness, our fears, and our foibles. Allowing ourselves to slip, to fall, to fail, even to make fools of ourselves every once in a while, and to bless our Selves anyway, despite our faults, or because of them.

My own discovery of the potent magic of Self-blessing came after I returned home from the agonizing months of my mother's deathwatch,

The Queen Suggests:
Take Your Coronation to Heart

Your heart is the symbol of your emotional Self. The arteries surrounding the heart are called "coronaries." Coronary, meaning "like a crown."

Before you crown your own head, take some time to connect with the wisdom of your heart. Sit in stillness until you can clearly envision the ideal Queen of your Self.

Cleanse your heart space with smudge. In the tradition of many tribes of Plains Indians, it is good to clear the Intentions in your heart with the smoke of burning sage. Cedar, frankincense, and camphor are also excellent agents of purification.

Pat your palm gently over your heart area to soothe, comfort, and encourage yourself, and to embrace your Self with your own love and support.

Rub your heart with the oil of myrrh, or smudge yourself with myrrh smoke. Myrrh is used to heal all old wounds to the heart, so that we might keep our heart chakra open and receptive without fear.

Touch your scepter to your heart, and then raise it on high, proclaiming your goals and intentions for the duration of your reign.

Put your hand on your heart and pledge allegiance to you. Announce your ordination loud and clear:

I am Queen Donna, Queen of My Self.

I am Queen Patricia, Queen of My Life.

I am Queen Deirdre, Queen of My Future.

I am Queen Daile, Queen of My Domain.

when I finally started to renew my long-repressed sense of Self-care and Self-help, and began to act conscientiously on my Intentions. Soon after my forty-ninth birthday Self-Consecration Ceremony, I developed the most startling predilection for congratulating myself every time I did the slightest positive thing for my Self. If I climbed the stairs instead of taking the elevator, for instance. If I handled a sticky situation well, or stuck up for my Self. If I remembered all of my vitamins, or if I really did drink eight glasses of water in a day without drowning, I would pat myself on the proverbial back and proclaim, "Good girl!"

This ritual was completely unconscious and it took weeks for me to even recognize that I was doing it. Once I did, though, it made me think. I remembered that I had never heard, "Good girl!" while I was growing up. I had always been the Not Good Enough Girl. But it also made me understand that now that my mother was gone, I would never again be subject to her scrutiny. Nor would I ever stand for anyone else speaking to me in a disrespectful way—including me. As Eleanor Roosevelt said, "Nobody can make you feel inferior without your permission." How many times have I told my dog that he is a good boy? A thousand times a day, I'm sure. Really, that's all I ever say to him. "Good boy, Bud. Come here, good boy. Sit, good boy. What a good boy. Bud is such a goooood boy." How many times had I said as much to *moi*? A recent survey reported that sixty-three percent of pet owners tell their animals that they love them every day. Would that we could love ourselves as much.

After awhile, it became clear that I was not actually congratulating myself. Rather, I was blessing my Self. What a good girl am I. How incredibly Queenly. The practice of my Self-blessing became my sacred daily ritual, the most holy of all my personal rites. Every morning I would look deeply into my eyes in the mirror and bless myself in order to help me to focus, facilitate, and enhance that mighty, internal energy-for-change that is my own best Self. The gift of Self-blessing is one that keeps on giving. The more I blessed myself, the more I blessed my Self. The more I valued

The Queen Suggests:
Crown Your Own Head with Blessings

There are two kinds of blessings: those that acknowledge and celebrate your growth and accomplishments, and those that proffer offerings of encouragement for that which you still hope to do.

Bless your Self as worthy. Congratulate your Self. Hug your Self close. Pat your Self on the back with pride. Pinch your own cheek with delight. Bow down and kiss your feet!

Bless your Self with words. It is important to articulate your blessing. Try verbalizing your thoughts out loud. Don't worry about what to say or how to say it. Speak to your deepest Self spontaneously, from your heart. There can be no such thing as a bad blessing. It is a contradiction in terms. If your Intention is positive, so will be your blessing.

Bless your Self with oil. Anoint the crown of your head with the Intention to concentrate on your Intention. My blessing enthusiasm led me to create a rainbow assortment of blessing oils —Green Juicy Fruits of Life for new beginnings, Magenta Carnal Arts for sensuality, Blue Calming Balm for peace of mind, Black Pitch of Night for working through sadness, Gold Leap of Faith for spiritual expansion — thirteen in all. Each unique blend in the collection was meant to resonate with one of my many diverse moods and desires and to encourage me to feed them as needed.

My assortment was formulated from essential oils, healing herbs, energy-charged gemstones, and colored glitter. Why not create your own special personalized blends to suit your needs?

Oils are not the only method of Self-blessing. The range of possibilities is as boundless as your imagination. Be specific, creative, and outrageous.

You can bless your Self every time you apply your lipstick. "I bless my Self. I bless what I put into my mouth and I bless what comes out of my mouth."

You can bless your Self with a scarf or a muffler. "I bless my Self. I wrap my Self with protection and surround my Self with love."

You can bless your Self with a sheet or blanket when you get into bed each night. "I bless my Self. I cover my Self with confidence, with affection, with appreciation, with support."

You can bless your Self with soap in the shower every morning. "I bless my Self. I cleanse my Self of impurities, insecurities, and all negative thinking."

You can bless your Self with unguents and lotions, applying them with loving affection. I bless my Self. I soothe and caress and embrace my Self and ease away all my troubles."

You can bless your Self each time you sneeze. "I bless my Self. Goddess bless me!"

The more you bless your Self, the more you believe it.
The more you believe it, the more you project it.
The more you project it, the more you attract it.

The Queen Suggests:
A Crowning Ceremony

Begin by inscribing a sacred circle to delineate the ritual space. You can use a visual marker such as chalk, flower petals, or ribbons. Or you can pass around oil or water or a musical instrument to create a circle outlined by smell, touch, taste, or sound. This space is safe and protected.

Introduce your intention. "This ceremony is to mark, to share, and to celebrate: My growth. My wisdom. My hard lessons. My changes. My odd achievements. My new beginnings."

What will you be leaving behind? "This is what I have created, nurtured, and loved." Bring your past into the circle. Create an altar filled with symbols that represent your past few decades. Light candles to remember them. Place on the altar pictures of your children, your parents, yourself. Your novel, your invention, your business ledger, your college diploma. Sanitary napkins and birth control devices. Acknowledge and honor them through story, song, poetry, movement, music, prayer. Put them down and let them go. Then, extinguish the candles.

Where are you now? "This is what I am feeling in this transition. These are my trials, my triumphs, my questions, and my fears: An empty nest. A loss of purpose. Putting on weight. Putting mom into a nursing home. Facing illness. Facing the future. Having enough money. Being alone. Falling apart. Falling in love again." You might do this part in the dark or blindfolded to represent your confusion and turmoil. Or by jumping up and down or spinning in circles to embody your turmoil.

Where are you going? "This is what I want for my Self, who I want to be." Create a second altar filled with items representing your desired future. You might want to dance or skip or run from the altar of the old to the altar of the new to symbolize your transition and ultimate transformation. Include objects that symbolize your empowered Self: Your crown. Your scepter. A blank notebook. An new businesscard, a student ID, a gym card. A travel guide. A new engagement calendar.

Welcome each item into your life and bless it for helping you conceive of and achieve your dreams. Light candles to illuminate your future.

Crown your Self Queen by declaring that it is so.

and validated my Self, the more compassionate toward my Self I became. The more worthy I felt, the more I trusted my Self, listened to my Self, and disciplined my Self. The more I blessed my Self, the more I counted my blessings, and the more blessed I, myself, became. Where blessing is concerned, more is definitely more.

For some ten years now, the practice of Self-blessing has been the centerpiece of many of the ceremonies and celebrations that I facilitate. When people are first introduced to the concept, they are often taken aback and suddenly shy. "Bless myself? Am I qualified? Isn't that blasphemy?" Surely we are each the most appropriate dispenser of our own blessings. Who, but we ourselves, really understands what we have been through, what we have gained and won, what we still need and desire, what we honor and aspire to? And who but we is dedicated to actualizing our own dreams? It is the spirit of Self-blessing that finally caps our journey toward Queendom and seals our transformation into sovereignty. Learning how to bless our Selves, and doing so often and without embarrassment, is truly our crowning achievement.

A CORONATION TO REMEMBER

When the Queen finally makes Her long-awaited appearance, Her attendance is unmistakable, unshakeable. We would know Her anywhere. She is just as we had hoped we could one day be. Better, even. The past has passed, and the future is full of the promise of our own passion and purpose. So, in appreciation and profound relief, we roll out the red carpet in royal welcome and salute Her with a coronation that befits Her station—a Crowning Ceremony in which we claim and celebrate our power for good, and give our Self the permission to use it. While the format of the ritual may differ, the ultimate intention of a Crowning Ceremony is always to mark the critical transition from our days as a Mother, biological or otherwise, to our time as a reigning Queen.

The Queen Suggests:
To Each Queen Her Own

A Coronation is no time for subtlety. Let your imagination run wild. You only become a Queen once.

Pomp and Circumstance. Have a Crowning Ceremony fit for a Queen. Make it dignified, regal, and high hat. Play baroque trumpet music, have a procession, scatter sparkly glitter, light golden candles. Have flower girls toss flower petals and curtsey sweetly. Serve honey mead and Marie Antoinette cake.

Cleopatra Spa Celebration. Set out lots of pillows for your guests to lounge on. Give each other facials, manicures, and pedicures. Henna your hair, hands, and feet. Decorate your eyes with kohl. Play dress up with harem pants and veils, pass out cymbals, do some belly dancing, and shake your sumptuous bootie. Serve figs and dates, nuts and sweetmeats, mint tea and Turkish coffee.

Mad Hatter Meets the Queen of Hearts Tea Party. Set the stage for a silly day. Encourage your guests and/or sister Queens to wear their most outrageous crowns and gowns. Toast and roast each other with poetic hilarity. Laugh at your Self. Trip the light fantastic. Serve sherry, endless cups of tea, and scones with clotted cream and jam.

Royal Wedding. Conduct a wedding for one. Declare yourself to your Self, to have and to hold, for better and for worse, till death do you part. Pledge to love, honor, and cherish your Self always. Have something old, something new, something borrowed, and something blue. Put a ring on your own finger. Hug and kiss your Self. Throw rice. Serve champagne, fancy hors d'oeuvres, and of course, delicious cake.

Amazon Queen Drum Circle. Prepare a lovely spot in nature. Outline a sacred circle with chalk, with candles, with ribbon, with garlands. Create an altar. Light a fire. Drum and chant and spin and dance in the moonlight. Bless each other, your Self, and the elements. Drum up the spirit of Goddess energy that links you to all the powerful female forces of the universe. Serve wine, fruit, cheese, and lovely circular loaves of bread.

My granddaughter Shameike once confided to me that she was "not the tutu type." Every Queen is not necessarily the ceremonial type, either. Every woman may not resonate with the idea of celebrating her new stage of life with a ritual. A Crowning Ceremony doesn't have to be literal to be a powerful and positive rite of passage into Queendom. There are any number of metaphors that can be employed to symbolize our transition. But one way or another, an occasion as momentous as achieving our sovereignty definitely deserves to be marked and honored in some well-considered way. We owe it to our Selves to celebrate our changes, our achievements, our memories, our hopes, and our glory, and to crown them with love.

When designing our ceremony, the Queen's Rules of Engagement apply: There are no rules, but only our best Intentions and our focused Attention. Everything else is frosting on the cake. We can design our moment any way we like in order for it to be personally relevant, as long as our Crowning Ceremony makes sacred our sense of Self-worth, proclaims our new role in life, and celebrates our successful ascendancy. As in any ritual, we should choose a special time and place, evocative décor, meaningful symbols, favorite music, and resonant words to read or recite. All of the details should reflect our Intention. The ceremony can be solo or shared among several Queens, perhaps in front of witnesses, and with or without someone to officiate.

Whatever the format, the theme, or the individual script, the intent and meaning is always the telling of the journey from Where I Was, to Where I Am Now, to Where I Am Going. This progression of life change can be symbolized in many allegorical ways: by the lighting, extinguishing, and re-lighting of candles, by a procession around the room from one altar to the next like stations of devotion, by dancing from one place to another, by taking off a garment and replacing it with a new one, by pouring water, like libations, from one container to another. The range of possibility for Crowning Celebration themes is infinite. Each of us can design an excellent rite to honor our passage that perfectly describes our particular-

The Queen Suggests:
Craft Your Own Crown

If you are new to arts and crafts, you can begin by purchasing a golden or silver cardboard party-favor crown to use as an armature. Then glue decorations onto it that reflect your particular regal fantasy and fashion sense. Here is your basic, classic, goes with anything, always-correct Queenly crown.

Or you can start from scratch and make your crown from craft materials such as wire, foil, tinsel, netting, ribbons, yarn, dried and silk flowers, beads, and sequins to adorn the ever-clever Queen of Creativity.

You can assemble a fantastical thrift store madcap crown created from scarves, boas, old hats, veils, jewelry, holiday ornaments, and assorted finds for the Camp Vamp Queen in you.

Or you can gather reeds, grasses, vines, seaweed, or other natural materials and weave a wreath from them. Add flowers, pinecones, twigs, shells, and feathers for that Queen Mother Earth look.

If tiaras aren't your thing, decorate a beret, a straw boater, or a baseball cap with special symbols of Your Royal Highness. Wear it with aplomb.

While you're at it, you might think about creating a scepter and a throne, as well.

journey, that speaks to our own beliefs, and that expesses our individual aesthetic.

If a Crowning Ceremony is meant to celebrate who we are now, we must include in that recognition who we once were, and the life we once knew. Our becoming has a herstory that begins before we were even born and extends back through the ages to the very beginning of time. Our culture, our heritage, our own life experience all contribute to form and inform us. Each person, place, and thing that we have ever encountered offers us teaching and enriches our being. Though we are sovereign, we are inextricably connected. Midlife is the perfect time to look back and assess our experiences, our memories, and our lessons, to see what we have done so far, where we have been, and who we have known, and to bless it all for being the basis of our becoming. Collecting the pieces and symbols that represent our lives to date and assembling them in some meaningful manner is a marvelous way to mark a change of life status. Creating art from our lives is a beautiful way to alter it, change it, embellish it, sanctify it, and carry it with us into the future.

Ultimately, we crown our Self with blessings. But an actual crown, especially one that we have made ourselves, can be a great reminder of our newly acquired royal status. Of course we can easily obtain a glittery rhinestone tiara, a crown suited for a beauty queen, a theatrical production, or a Mardi Gras costume. But how much more meaningful to create our own ourselves. We have crafted our own lives, after all, why not create a crown to fit our unique and particular specifications? Our crown is the visible badge of our authority, and making it is an excellent meditation on what it means for us to claim our Queendom. How will the circumstances of our lives change? How will our intentions and attitudes be altered? How will our outward demeanor and expression evolve? What impression do we intend to create? What kind of Queens are we to become?

The Queen Suggests:
Crown Your Memories

Create a scrapbook. Collect your memorabilia into a lovely blank book. Decorate the pages with colored ink, glitter, stickers, and emblems as you did when you were a child. Make collages, drawings, and prints. Add your favorite quotations and affirmations for inspiration.

Create a quilt. Collect fabric from old clothes that hold good memories. Use your own and ask for something from those whom you love. Cut the clothes into pieces and stitch them together in a patchwork pattern. Make a pillow or duvet case, or a robe, a sacred vestment, to cover and surround your Self with all the collected energy that they contain.

Create a mosaic project. Collect all the little bits and pieces that you have held onto forever because of their sentimental value. Souvenirs of nature trips, such as seashells, stones, and seed pods along with broken china and jewelry, assorted beads, and buttons can be cemented onto a vase, a bowl, a picture frame, a bird bath, a bathroom wall, to create a three-dimensional personal portrait.

A Crowning Achievement

Another popular way of marking our passage into Queendom is to perform some remarkable feat or undertake an awesome adventure to prove strength of body, mind, and spirit. I once entertained the fantasy of walking the entire length of the Appalachian Trail in celebration of my midlife transition. Alas, when the time came, I found myself somewhat short on enthusiasm at the prospect of undertaking such an ambitious physical commitment—without several attending Sherpas, that is. I have never been much of an athlete, but my friend Cristina succeeded in climbing Mt. Kilimanjaro on her fiftieth birthday, a compelling metaphor for ascending into her mastery. Janet hiked the Milford track in New Zealand on her fiftieth. When she was fifty-five, Evelyn swam for the first time across the sizeable lake that fronted her cottage in Maine, and Alice jumped out of an airplane in her mid-sixties, when she felt that she had reached the peak of her powers.

I have recently encountered an entire body of literature documenting the midlife travels of women who have journeyed out into the world in order to discover its wonders as well as their own. These Queens of the Road use travel as an allegory, a moving meditation, on passing into a new period of life. Rita Golden Gelman, for example, took a two-month experimental "break" from her marriage when she was in her mid-forties, which she describes in her book, *Tales of a Female Nomad*. Her kids off to college, she decided to go to Mexico to discover what was missing in her life, a major adventure for someone who had never so much as gone to a restaurant alone. Her exploratory trip turned into a nearly two-decade-long solo tour of the world. In *Living on Wilderness Time,* Melissa Walker, a professor and the mother of grown children, tells about taking off into the wilderness soon after her fiftieth birthday to explore first-hand the environmental theories that she taught in her college classes. Walker's travels served to solidify her marriage and set her onto a new career path.

The Queen Suggests:
Crown Your Accomplishments

Do something new.

Do something differently.

Do something hard.

Do something easy, but do it more often.

Do something that scares or challenges you.

Do something that you have been putting off.

Do something completely out of character.

Do something wonderful anonymously.

Do something simple.

Do something silly.

Do something grand.

Do something meaningful.

The Queen Suggests:
Crown Your Aspirations

Plant a tree, a flowering bush, or a vegetable garden.

Make a list of your hopes, wishes, desires, and goals for the future. Fold these intentions into a tiny bundle, and bury it beneath the roots of what you have planted. Your dreams will take root, grow, bud, leaf, flower, and fruit along with the plant.

Make another list of everything old and negative that you would like to leave behind as you go your Queenly way. Burn this list in a pot. Powder the ash and sprinkle it on your plants. You are feeding the future with the lessons of your past mistakes.

If this is midlife, where we have come from and who we have been is only half of the picture. Our Crowning should culminate with our looking forward toward the future. If each beauty queen contestant in the Miss America Pageant must answer the question of where she will apply her Queenly Intentions and Attention during her reign, so, certainly, must we. Where do we go from here? To what will we dedicate our energy? How will we use our power? What will we do? Build? Change? Rule? And how will we do it?

We have come a long way and it has been quite a journey. We have dreamed the dream, done the work, and walked the long, long highway. We have struggled to discover, comfort, cosset, encourage, and change our Selves. And we have crowned our best Intentions, Attention, and efforts, our accomplishments, lessons, and aspirations. Now, finally, gloriously, joyfully, we have arrived at our destination: the station of our authentic sovereignty. And don't it feel grand?

Affirmation of All That I Have Lived and Seen So Far

You know what?
I like myself.
I trust myself.
I know myself.
I know what I want.
I know what I need.
I know what I have.
I know what I know.
I mean well.
I try hard.
I do good.
I help.
I heal.
I hear.
I love.
I feel.
I fall down.
I stand up.
I strive.
I survive.
I flourish.
I thrive.

—D.H.

CHAPTER 7

Royal Flush

STRUTTING OUR STUFF

*A strong woman is a woman who loves
strongly, and weeps strongly, and is
strongly terrified and has strong needs.*
—Marge Piercy, American author and poet (1936-)

I have pretty much always had a current love interest, a paramour, an inamorata-of-the-moment in my life. Ever since elementary school, I have been involved in a series of crushes, flirtations, romances, relationships, and marriage/partnerships of varying degrees of consummation, duration, maturity, intensity, and pleasure. However, before I turned fifty, I had never felt myself to be particularly beautiful in the abstract. While I had definitely attracted my share of admirers, one by one, over the decades, it is not as though I ever had a queue of suitors waiting outside my front door, vying for my affection. Try though I might, I never quite fit the popular, idealized, mass-market parameters of beauty or body type or demeanor. Far from being a femme fatale with a Hollywood face or figure, I usually failed to turn heads in a crowd.

Certainly I had been told many times that I was pretty, but it was always in the dubious context of, "You really ought to lose some weight, you have such a pretty face." Or, "Why don't you pull your hair off your face so that people can see you." Those motherly suggestions didn't exactly serve as Self-image enhancing morale-builders. Oh, I was probably pretty enough, but it was a pasted-on look. My lips were fetchingly colored, but my smile was frozen in fear. During the Maiden years of my teens and twenties, I was serious, withdrawn, self-conscious, over-sensitive, and as unsure as a tentative spring shoot caught in an inclement frost.

Completely unprepared emotionally, I was out there and available because I was expected to be. But my heart was never in it. I was way too shy to perceive—let alone enjoy, and heaven forbid, show—myself as the sweet, loving, sensual, sexual, swan-in-waiting that I really was in my secret, tender hidden heart. Instead of feeling good about who I was, I believed and internalized everything that I had been taught: that I was not thin enough, striking enough, or vivacious enough to attract appreciative attention. And that was what life was supposed to be all about, after all, wasn't it girls?

COMING INTO OUR OWN

And then, a remarkable thing happened. This ugly duckling grew and changed as if magically transformed. The more I explored the world around me, the more I learned about myself. The more I searched for experience and meaning outside of me, the more I discovered that I liked what I found inside. The more excited by life that I felt, the more attractive and exciting I, in turn, became. Because I felt more and more sure of myself, sure of my path and my purpose, I became less guarded and more open. Because I had learned how to be safe in my own care, I felt more trusting, less defended, and much less defensive. Something in me had thawed. My withholding tension released. Without realizing it, I had been holding my breath for years, "waiting to exhale," as Terry McMillan put it in her novel of the same title. Now, I had nothing to hide.

When I burst forth from the springtime of my Maidenhood into my summer Mother Time almost a quarter of a century ago, I discovered that I was a bud turned blossom. I had flowered into an adult woman—creative, productive, and nurturing—Mother of Invention, foster Mother to lost children and animals, practicing artist, spiritual adventurer, author of my Self. The power of attraction, seduction, and sex was suddenly, for the very first time, in my court. As a Maiden, I would sometimes date people simply because they asked me out, whether I really wanted to be with them or not. I was *that* flattered. But as I entered my thirties and early forties, my longings and lust began to come more directly out of my own desires. It took a long time and much introspective effort, but I grew to know my wants and my needs, emotionally and sexually. After a decades-long struggle, I had come to believe in my right to act upon my own desires and to expect them to be honored.

We have to dare to be ourselves, however frightening or strange that self may prove to be.
—*May Sarton, American author and poet (1912-1995)*

That hard-won Self-knowledge and acceptance has only grown more intense and powerful as my once-luscious bloom has ripened into fruitful age. Now that I have entered my autumn years of Queendom, I have become a well-seasoned woman, mature and plump and ready for the picking. Piquant, tart, sweet, succulent, and juicy, ripe with the cycle of life, I am what my Chicana friend Linda calls *Una mujer in su salsa*. A hot sauce woman. Relaxed and contracted in the Fire Queen's sweltering heat, I'm slower now, and surer, like thick crystallized syrup. Honey made for me, the Queen Bee, from the wildflower I once was. I'm strong and steady, salty and spicy, oh, so sultry, if a little bit dusty. A little wrinkled. A little weary. A little saggy, a little worn. But infinitely stronger, steadier, and a whole lot wiser. I bear the fruits of my own labors, and I wear them well.

After coming through my trying times of midlife loss, those painful years of upsets, setbacks, detours, and challenges met and learned from, I am now fully charged with my Self and very much in charge. By working deeply and diligently on my own transformation into the Queen of my Self, I have reached an unexpected level of contentment and confidence and I am savoring every second of it. I know there is no time to waste. Like any Queen, I do not squander the harvest of my valuable resources, nor do I underestimate my own worth. I have passed into the majesty of proud maturity. And it shows. This is surely what they mean by PMV (post-menopausal vigor and vim). Radiant, I am lit from within.

My period of healing Self-absorption had a thrilling aphrodisiac effect—from the inside out. I felt attractive and sexy, therefore I was. My entire Self was charged with new confidence and ease of being: my head held high with pride and Self-esteem; my eyes alive with what I had seen, the many sights and insights; my cheeks red from the chase—and hair to match. I was a mean, clean, spirit-driven machine, shined with spit and polish, full of gas, revved and ready to go. How attractive is that? Now, "Who's the fairest of them all?"

And I am not alone. In Joyce Tenneson's wonderful book of photographic portraits, *Wise Women,* one of the lovely women who she interviewed expressed the sort of new-found knowledge of herself as a powerfully attractive older woman that I've come to recognize in many other women my age and older. "People often stop me now and tell me I'm beautiful," says Betty Silverstein. "I never had that happen when I was younger. So for me aging has, at least on the surface, made others more interested in me and who I am." Marilyn Alex, another older woman who Tenneson profiles, proclaims, "I think it's cool being older—I still get hit on. People are always telling me how beautiful I am now. It's like they are almost incredulous because the old stereotype is that we shouldn't get more beautiful with age. I have respect for the body and live in harmony with nature;

that's where beauty comes from."

A new view of a powerful, sexual, spirited, and successful middle-aged woman is becoming ever more visible in popular culture. Tens of millions strong, women now entering midlife are busily engaged in the process of rewriting the rules of beauty, style, and sexiness as we explore, express, and celebrate the diverse parameters of our own individual appeal. We have always been independent of thought, adventurous, and courageous, daring to experiment despite traditional convention and condemnation. We have established career networks, circles of friends, emotional, spiritual, and material support systems upon which we can depend. Since we no longer need a mate to provide for us, we can engage as equals. We have worked hard to achieve a sense of Self-sufficiency and continue to strive for a state of peace and love within our Selves. This strong center of confidence empowers us to connect with others with candor and compassion.

OUR BODIES, OUR SELVES

It matters more what's in a woman's face than what's on it.
—Claudette Colbert, American actress (1903-1996)

As we age, we naturally change. The Queen knows change to be the essential stuff of life and embraces it with magnanimous grace and good humor, as part and parcel of the ongoing mythic adventure of Her life. She is a traveler on the royal road to Her own best Self. Like most women, I can't help but notice the parts that have slumped and sagged as I've aged. The bags under my eyes now have overnight valises of their own. The veins in my legs and on the backs of my hands are starting to show through in blue. And forget my figure. Everything not tied down has long since fallen:

my breasts, my belly, my once taut neck. I can easily commiserate with the South African writer Nadine Gordimer, who once commented, "I'm forty-nine but I could be twenty-five except for my face and legs."

Now, I love the fact that we lose our vision and our youthful beauty at the same time. What we can't see can't hurt us. It is a brilliant kindness to our vanity that reinforces in me the belief that God is surely a Goddess. As I squint at myself in the mirror while I try to keep my lipstick confined to the general vicinity of my lips, I think "Well, hey, I don't look so bad!" I just know that I am going to be one of those old ladies with bright cockatiel orange circles of rouge on my cheeks and lipstick half up to my nose. Beauty is all in the eyes of the beholder, after all—the blinder to flaws the better.

*It gets easier as you get older. You accept yourself.
for who you are—your flaws and your attributes.
It's easier to live in your own skin.*
—*Barbra Streisand, American singer, actor,
producer, director (1940-)*

But recognizing and accepting the inevitability of aging does not mean giving up on any attempts at improving our outward appearance, physical health, mental outlook, emotional balance, and general well-being. More than ever before, women of a certain age are taking better care of our Selves, conscious of a newly mature imperative to lovingly nurture and protect every aspect of our beings. We accept the responsibility for our own sustenance and satisfaction: physically as well as mentally, emotionally, and spiritually. My sister midlifers—many of us for the first time ever—are pursuing programs of nutrition and fitness. We are eating better, sleeping and exercising more, learning how to release our stress, pursuing spiritual connection, and allowing ourselves to fully express our creative natures.

We are working hard to stay healthy and active, and are, at the same time, more realistic in our ideals, more accepting of our own perceived imperfections, and more forgiving of our weaknesses. While some of us do go to the starvation-botox-surgical-extremes of trying to stay forever young, in general, we follow fewer fad diets and adopt more sensible, sustainable, and ultimately successful life-style changes. We gradually heal ourselves of old destructive patterns, stinking thinking, and nasty habits. And then, voila! The rewarding result of feeling well—inside and out—is looking well. Astrid Bedrossian, of the famous Georgette Klinger Salon in New York City says, "Women who come to us look better than ever before. They take care of themselves with intelligence. Beauty for them is increasingly linked to looking healthy."

Of all the physical tokens of my aging, the one I have minded the most is my wrinkled neck. My mother used to hate her neck, too, and only wore shirts and sweaters with high necklines. On many occasions when I felt especially self-conscious, I would stand in front of the mirror and pull the extra skin back and up toward my ears with my fingers to simulate the "after" picture in an advertisement for face-lifts. The technique does, indeed, make you look younger, but not necessarily better. All that shrink-wrapping erases any trace of emotion from the face, leaving a portrait devoid of animation. A radiant smile, I have discovered, is a much more effective beauty treatment. Not only do I look better, more alert, curious, connected, and alive, but smiling also works its magic from the outside in and makes me feel much better.

Queens that we are, we understand that there is a difference between looking young and looking attractive—between, for that matter, looking attractive and *being* attractive. The striking results of a recent poll of midlife women showed that almost forty-eight percent of the respondents were "completely" satisfied and another forty-four percent were "somewhat" satisfied by the way they looked "for their age." That is an astonishing ninety-two percent in all! Nearly nine out of ten women—

The Queen Suggests:
Let Your Light Shine Through

Stand or sit comfortably in front of a mirror. Close your eyes. Allow your face to relax and go completely slack. Let your expression and eyes be absolutely blank.

Don't smile. Don't frown. Try not to show any emotion at all. Open your eyes and look at yourself honestly, but without judgement. Notice how your face sags and how dull your eyes appear. And yes, how haggard you look.

Now close your eyes again and imagine that you are at a social occasion and are engaged in a lively discussion with people that you like. Tell yourself a joke and laugh out loud. Open your eyes.

Do you see how a little humor and joy animates your entire visage? Your eyes are suddenly sparkling. Your cheeks are raised and your neck is much more taut. You look happy and vibrant and very appealing. And of course, you feel as good as you look, because the act of smiling actually produces a chemical reaction in the brain that releases mood enhancing endorphin-like hormones.

Goddess help me, but my mother was right. You do attract more flies with honey than with vinegar. The Queen Bee ought to know.

eighty-eight percent—indicated that they were pleased with their appearance, period, age not being a factor. But even while these women were generally so accepting of their appearance, the study revealed that the highest priorities of these women as they aged were internal. Ninety-five percent of them said that feeling good about themselves was "essential."

It is only a disaster to lose our girlish charms if we deem them to be the exclusive path to beauty, love, and fulfillment. In many of my circles, I've listened to women who have come to not only accept but to celebrate their own process of aging. Tesse, an X-ray technician from upstate New York, is married to a man who is a good deal older than she is. When they were first married twenty years ago, her husband told her that a young woman couldn't hold a candle to the beauty of a forty-five-year-old. This used to bother her intensely. Although it was clear to her that he has loved her very much all these years, now that she has finally reached forty-five and has begun to mourn the loss of her youthful beauty, his attentions are more arduous than ever, which has eased her fears of aging.

Our allure and sex appeal change with time—increase, even—if we allow them to. A woman is never too old to look and feel beautiful. Each age, each stage in our lives, has its particular fabulous charm. In her fascinating book, *Notes on the Need for Beauty*, J. Ruth Gendler writes, "It seems so obvious that if we really appreciated what a gift it is to be alive in our bodies and how amazingly complex and intricate these bodies are, we wouldn't be able to hate ourselves so well. We would recognize our own beauty not in an arrogant way, but simply as part of the beauty in this amazing world. Just imagine if all the talent in advertising that went into convincing us that we aren't good enough, could be freed for true creative work."

When someone told Gloria Steinem that she didn't look forty, she famously replied, "This is how forty looks." And that goes double now that she is in her sixties. The Queen refuses to condescend or conform to the adolescent and exploitative standard of beauty promulgated by popular culture. She does not deign to compare herself with teenage models or emaciated-lifted-stitched-tucked-injected Hollywood *über*-beauties. "Acknowledging the body is acknowledging what is real. It is such a strain, a struggle, to appear to be without physical blemish," observed the author, painter, and playwright, Roslyn Drexler, "to remain young as the relentless years add up. It's time consuming and emotionally depleting."

A truly mature, secure woman accepts the inevitable physical changes that come with the passing of time and incorporates them into the way she presents herself to the world. Self-aware, Self-assured, she transforms her Self as she goes. She glows as she grows into her full potential, and becomes ever more becoming. Her reinvigorated attractiveness stems from Self-knowledge and enfranchisement; her magnetic sensuality is centered in the fulfillment and satisfaction of her Self-worth. She exudes the intoxicating appeal of a woman who is, at heart, pleased with her Self.

It's unbecoming for an old broad to sing about how bad she wants it. But occasionally we do.
—Lena Horne, American singer and actress (1917-)

WHAT'S SEX GOT TO DO WITH IT?

When I began this journey toward my Self, I was an innocent in many respects. Responsible beyond my years, yet repressed, compressed, regressed, like the tightest pussy willow—the one with the hardest shell—protection for my fuzzy, fertile possibility. Eventually, the storms of change and loss that I faced during my tumultuous maternal years had weathered my once-sumptuous bloom. Like many women of a certain age, I had gradually, imperceptibly almost, let myself go, like an overblown rose clinging inside out to the vine in the fall, my petals ratty, and my rose hips growing ever rounder. Of all that we stand to lose in the aging process, the waning of our sexual attraction and appeal is perhaps for many of us, the scariest prospect of all.

But this assumption goes against all evidence of the actual midlife experiences of many women, my own included. "It's funny," my fifty-three-year-old friend Judith confided to me over coffee. "I am making peace with my appearance these days and I find that I don't really care about what people might think or say about the way I look. I am confident of myself for the first time in my life. Sometimes I catch myself making eye contact —even flirting—with men, something I would never have done when I was younger. Men often look at me with appreciation, too, when I least expect it. I know I feel good in myself and I have fun and flaunt it. I guess I must look fine too, but in a different way."

According to sexuality experts, women in our forties are just coming into the ascendancy of our sexual powers, with decades of pleasures to look forward to. In a recent survey conducted by *Living Fit* magazine, fifty percent of women declared that menopause increased their sexual desire and thirty-five percent were pleased to announce that their orgasms had become more intense. "All I have to say," gushed Luz, a high school teacher in one of my Queen Workshops, "is that it just gets better and better for me. I am forty-four-years old and I feel like I am just getting going." The noted sexuality educator Betty Dodson agrees. "I've been postmenopausal for two decades and I'm having spectacular orgasms alone and with a partner," she writes.

After five decades of rather modest, but satisfyingly enjoyable sex appeal ratings, I found that when I reached my fifties, I was suddenly turning heads wherever I went. The Queen that I had become began to attract super-charged affection and lustful admiration from friends and strangers alike. Like bees to a hive, an electric attention buzzed around me, tickling my Self-perceived image, stroking my Sex Goddess ego. Lush with lust, supreme in my creative powers of seduction and fulfillment, I identified with the great lineage of Love and Fertility Goddesses who have been revered throughout time and culture. Their power, raw and electric, was their Self-knowledge, their exquisite access to ecstasy, their generative heat, their sex, the seat of their strength. The vitality, the powerful intensity of their sheer desire, their boundless energy, was potent enough to produce generations, poetry, agriculture, science, art, and craft. The same fire, the same hot love that ignites to spark the beginning of babies, also kindles the creation of culture. Their hunger was the force that fashioned all life, and their love the fuel that maintained it.

This primal sexuality was imbued with spiritual significance. Sex, especially the female experience of it, has been all but universally invoked in myth and ritual as symbolic of the primary force, the fiery source of life. For the Goddesses of Love and Life, unabashed and bold, sex was an authentic religious expression. Sex as energy. Sex as celebration. Sex as creation. Sex as abundance. Sex as unification. Sex as divine spirit. Sex as sympathetic magic. In my newly recovered sensuality, I, too, was the Queen Bee, Aphrodite, Nefertiti, Cleopatra, the beautiful black Queen of Sheba. Honey, I was the Queen of Hearts.

My vulva, the horn.
The Boat of Heaven
Is full of eagerness like the moon
My untilled land lies fallow

As for me, Inanna,
Who will plow my vulva?
Who will plow my high field?
Who will plow my wet ground?
—Inscription on a Sumerian clay tablet (2000 BC)

I first noticed this startling new effect when I began to get wolf whistles from construction crews and guys in passing cars. Each time it happened, it shocked me deeply. What in the world? I am old enough to be these guys' mother. I thought that those kinds of experiences were long over for me. "Wow!" I would secretly marvel, "I never thought I would hear *that* again." Whereas in the past, I would react with the rage of a scorned Amazon at such macho street behavior, I suddenly found it to be flattering. I felt terrifically gratified in a totally guilt-ridden unfeminist sort of way.

One night recently I was stopped at a traffic light in my car, on my way home from an evening spent with friends. It had been a wonderful occasion and I was bathed in mellow pleasure. When I happened to turn my head to the left, I saw that the extremely handsome thirty-something-year-old man in the car next to me was trying to catch my eye. He flirted with me in a rather sophisticated and urbane Cary Grantish style, and I burst out laughing at the absurdity of it. He laughed then. And for that moment we made a real connection, direct and human, person-to-person, soul-to-soul, across the artificial barriers of age, gender, and race. Attraction is simply energy sent and received. Good energy is the spice of life.

How can any deny themselves the pleasure
of my company? It's beyond me.
—Zora Neale Hurston, American writer
and folklorist (1903-1960)

A Lot of Hot Women

Many women now entering midlife have always been pleasure seekers. Our generation created and experienced the Sexual Revolution, after all. And we are not likely to stop now, thank you very much. The time

The Queen Suggests:
Anoint Your Self for Pleasure

For some women, the noticeable reduction in vaginal fluid during menopause is a sexual deterrent, as it may take longer to become aroused and penetration may become irritating. But a little dryness down there doesn't stop the lusty Queen. That's why the Goddess invented cocoa butter.

Unguents and lotions and moisturizing potions are really quite sexy. Experiment with commercial lubricants or try rubbing yourself with some honey, fragrant coconut cream, almond, walnut, avocado, or olive oil, sweet Danish butter, molasses, chocolate syrup, or whatever tickles your fancy. Think of it as a way of blessing yourself with the power of your own pleasure.

for loving has never been better. By midlife, many of us who have had kids are now liberated from the constraints of child rearing and can afford the uninterrupted time and energy to attend unabashedly to our sex lives. Heterosexual sex, finally divorced from any worries or pressures of pregnancy, is now enjoyed simply for its own sake, pleasure rather than procreation as its motivation. As Virginia Woolf observed, "The older one grows the more one likes indecency." We are completely free to indulge ourselves in the joys of seduction, intimacy, sensuality, passion, and satisfaction.

"I feel sexier than ever," confided Margie, a fifty-one-year-old financial consultant, to the other women in a recent Queen Workshop. "But even though I have been having more opportunities than usual, I am not looking for a partner. I just feel hot and happy all over with the excitement of starting a new phase of my life. And the weird thing is that it's better than sex. You know?" "Ooh, yeah, I know just what you mean," piped in Laurie, a painter who is fifty-eight. "Being alone in my studio, creating work that consumes me, is such a turn-on. I masturbate all the time these days. It is fantastic. I haven't been at it like this since I was in my teens and just discovering the pleasure. But it is so much more powerful now. Such a charge." When the Queen takes responsibility for Her life, She controls Her own sexual experience whether it is solo, with another woman, or with a man. We are the Queens of Fire, after all. Our fervor is reaching the boiling point and our inhibitions are melting away in the heat of our rekindled passion for life. We are asizzle with ourselves.

By middle age, we have come to know who we are. We know what we like and we know how to get it. As in every other area of Her existence, the Queen cannot tolerate living in any way that constricts the expression of Her true nature and desires. She assumes responsibility for Her own enjoyment and makes sure that Her sensual and emotional needs are met. Most important of all, we are more inclined now to go out and manifest what we want. In her recent book, *A Round-Heeled Woman*, Jane Juska describes her own late-in-life flowering. She was in her mid-sixties when

The Queen Suggests:
Play with Fire

Regular sex, according to medical research, has the same benefits as regular exercise. It increases the flow of certain chemicals that naturally boost and strengthen the immune system, improves cholesterol levels, stimulates circulation, invigorates the heart, diminishes the intensity of pain, especially in migraines and chronic arthritis, reduces PMS symptoms, and releases endorphins which simply make you feel good.

Physical Sex. Make friends with your body. The more accepting you are of your physical being—your best features as well as your flaws—the more comfortable you will be sharing it. Develop your sense of touch. Cover the surface of your body with paint, with clay, with cream, with silk. Caress the textures. Feel the tactile sensations on your skin. Treat yourself to a massage, a manicure, or a facial. Pat, stroke, rub, knead your skin and hair. Offer to massage someone. Ask someone to do it for you.

Appreciate your body. Know that this body allows you to participate fully in life. Don't take this tremendous gift for granted. Express your gratitude for its durability, dependability, and recuperative powers. Bless the feet that take you where you want to go, the back that holds you upright, the hands that serve you so well, the eyes that you see out of, the heart that keeps on ticking. Bless your life in its physical form and enjoy it.

Treat your body well. Feed it wisely, air it often, water and exercise it with Intention and care. Pay Attention to its proper maintenance and upkeep. Keep it oiled and greased and limber, and don't let it get rusty. Nurture its need to be nurtured. Tend to its requirements and pamper all of its parts. Prepare your body for sex. Soak in a warm tub full of fragrant water to melt into the mood. Rub luscious lotion all over yourself, caressing each mound and crevice and curve with love and anticipation.

Mental Sex. Mind your memories, good and bad. Do not dwell in the past. Do not look back in time in order to yearn for more youthful days or compare yourself today with who you used to be. And do not let past pain, rejection, repression, or abuse deprive you of your present pleasures. Deal with what you want to change so that you can Be Here Now.

Mind your manners. Be nice. Be kind. Be patient. Be encouraging, but be sure to ask for what you want. Be willing to communicate with an open ear as well as with an open mouth. Be clear and specific. Be gentle, but firm. Speak your truth and expect to be heard. Share your desires and fantasies and play them out. Show and tell.

Mind your P's and Q's. P stands for permission. Allow yourself to follow your instincts and your desires and give yourself the unconditional permission to do what comes naturally, whatever that might mean to you. Q is for the Queen in you who knows what She likes. And She knows how to get it.

Emotional Sex. Explore the full range of your sexual emotions. What feelings does sex engender in you? What needs do you want it to fill? Does it? Is sex an outlet for the release of stress, of anger, frustration, or boredom? Is it an avenue to tenderness, affection, closness, intimacy, honesty, safety, openness, trust, and love?

Express your true emotional Self in all its myriad moods. Allow your funny, silly, lazy, sad, colorful, soulful, sinful parts out to play. Be adventurous. Be bold. Be brazen. Be wild. Be inventive. Don't worry, the kids won't be able to hear you. Be silent. Be solo. Be celibate. Be whatever you damn well please.

Exorcise your demons. Relax your resistance. Release your inhibitions. Let go of your mind altogether. Forget your emotions and all of your mental ramblings for a while, and just let yourself be. There are times when it is important to reflect upon and connect with your thoughts and feelings, and there are times when it's just as beneficial to disengage. Sex would be one of those times to let go.

Spiritual Sex. Create a sexual sanctuary, a safe and sacred space, a Temple of Love in which to indulge in your pleasures. Remove all distracting items that relate to the other parts of your life: notebooks, briefcases, pagers, bills, calendars. Turn the phones off, including the cell at the bottom of your purse. Cover the clocks. Close the bathroom door.

Smudge your space with the smoke of myrrh or copal to cleanse the atmosphere and with the smoke of sweetgrass to invite in the sweet spirits. Create a mood conducive to enchantment, enticement, and enjoyment. This is the royal boudoir, after all. A Garden of 1001 Delights. Decorate it in such a way as to appeal to all of the senses. Sheets and covers in soft fabrics: chenille, flannel, satin, to lie upon. Candles, soft lights, colored walls, flowers, and objets of art to please the gaze. Evocative perfumes, oils, and incense to smell. Lovely treats to taste.

Create a ritual before you make love. Think of sex as a way to connect, alone or in company, with the vibrating *Kundalini* energy that courses through you and the entire universe. Sanctify and ignite your Intention by lighting a candle, saying a prayer, or by singing, chanting, drumming, dancing, anointing. Reach out to engage your Self, another, and All That Is, in an ecstatic embrace of spirit, passion, and love.

she came to realize that she has never enjoyed a really exciting, fulfilling love affair. She had come from a repressed midwestern background and suffered through a loveless marriage and decades in social retreat while she was a single mom. When she finally passed through her midlife changes, she took matters into her own hands and took out a personal ad in *The New York Review of Books*. "Before I turn sixty-seven next March, I would like to have a lot of sex with a man I like." Chronicling her comic adventures, Juska writes, "Life just keeps coming at you… but every so often, you can catch a piece of it and make it do what you want it to, at least for a little while."

Our new take-charge sexual attitude can be just the catalyst needed to refuel the lethargic passion of our long-term marriage or partnership, or it could send us out in other, sometimes completely unexpected, directions. We could decide to take a lover, or a different lover, or an additional lover. If we have long been single, we might decide to begin dating and establishing relationships. We might, as is becoming more and more common, liberate our previously hidden, unfulfilled yearnings and "come out" as a lesbian in midlife. Or, if we have always been sexually active, involved and/or coupled, we could choose a period of celibacy, Self-exploration, Self-indulgence, and Self-love. The world is our oyster and we pick and choose according to our own persuasion.

A Beautiful Mind

A positive attitude is a Self-fulfilling prophecy cycle. When we look good, we feel good and when we feel good, we look great. The brain, the mind, is said to be our most sensitive sexual organ. Time after time, I have seen that being in possession of a vivacious, fully engaged, energized personality is much more enticing and erotic than having an outwardly pretty face or perfectly honed physique. It seems to me that the popular misperception that midlife marks the end of a woman's sexuality, her attraction and appeal, has less to do with her losing her looks than her losing her way, her sense of adventure, her enthusiasm, her spirit, her relationship with her Self. Allure is visceral and shines from within.

There is a fountain of youth: it is your mind, your talents, the creativity you bring to your life and the lives of the people you love. When you learn to tap this source, you will truly have defeated age.
—Sophia Loren, Italian actress (1934-)

While our bodies do, undeniably, change as we get older, so do our minds, our experiences, our attitudes, our expectations, and our priorities. We no longer judge nor allow ourselves to be judged by appearance alone. We do not seek to emulate or compete with others and are content to be our Selves. We even learn to love our so-called flaws. "I really like my wrinkles," my sixty-three-year-old friend Sharon told me. "I think they are sexy. They tell my story like the highway lines on a map. I have earned every one of them and have learned so much in the process." Terese, an ex-model feels the same way about her silver-gray hair. "It makes me look and feel very distinguished, like I am being taken seriously. That's what they say about middle-aged men with gray hair, and it is true for women, too." Jesse, the thirty-two-year-old husband of a fifty-year-old woman, explained to me recently why he admires the beauty of middle-aged women. "They care about how they present themselves to the world, but their presence and loveliness is not dictated by their physical attributes only. Their self-confidence makes them hard to resist."

In midlife we have the opportunity to reinvent ourselves. To create a way of being in the world that honors our most basic inner needs and expresses our confidence and individuality. More and more, we liberate ourselves from the expectations of others, choosing to please our Selves, instead. This applies to all aspects of our lives—our relationships, our families, our careers, our physical and mental health, our hearts and our spirits.

The Queen uses the power of Her own purpose, growth, and gratification to claim and proclaim what is rightfully Hers, including—especially—Her own Self-image, charisma, and sexuality. When we are comfortable in our own skin, we carry ourselves with presence and pride, and project our formidable inner beauty for all to see and appreciate. "Sex appeal is fifty percent what you've got," advises Sophia Loren, "and fifty percent what people think you've got." How we see and allow ourselves to be in our middle years will not only direct the course of our lives today, it will affect generations of younger women and girls who will follow in our regal footsteps.

Our emotional maturity and depth of character make women in our middle years extraordinarily and vitally attractive. We are substantial and robust, heady with the flavor of all that we have seen and done so far. We are pungent with profound experience, with pain and loss, exploration and transformation, glory and joy. The myriad lessons learned from lives intensely lived are reflected in our palate, which has become sophisticated, subtle, firm, and complex. Like fine wine and good cheese, women ripen and improve with age. Our essence becomes stronger, clearer, and infinitely more powerful. What could be more sexy?

For attractive lips, speak words of kindness.
For lovely eyes, seek out the good in people.
For a slim figure, share your food with the hungry.
For beautiful hair, let a child run his fingers
through it once a day. For poise, walk with
the knowledge that you never walk alone.
—Audrey Hepburn, Belgian-born
American actress (1929-1993)

A short while ago I came out of a business meeting full of excitement about the prospect of working on a fascinating new project and also about my own ability to pursue it. My outlook was optimistic and animated, and my outfit wasn't bad, either. I suppose I must have been smiling to myself as I strode through the rush hour crowds clogging the Herald Square subway platform. When the train finally pulled up, a man standing ahead of me stepped aside rather than enter the car before me. He twirled around, bowed, and with a grand flourish, ushered me into the car. I swear if he had had a cloak, he would have laid it at my feet for me to trod upon. A regular Sir Galahad of 34th Street, which would make me the Queen.

Astonished, I nodded my appreciation to him and stepped into the jammed subway car. Then, miracle of all miracles, a young man stood up and in a truly chivalric manner offered me his seat. Such courtliness would have been rare enough had I been hobbling on crutches, eight months pregnant, or eighty-years old. But his response to me was not one of pity. He was acting out of some primal attraction to a charismatic mature female power, some presence of stature that he sensed within me. Both of these men had afforded me courtly honor. And I could not have felt more like a Queen that afternoon if I had been wearing a wide brimmed turquoise hat, white gloves, and little black purse.

A woman in harmony with her spirit is like a river flowing. She goes where she will without pretense and arrives at her destination prepared to be herself and only herself.
—*Maya Angelou, American writer and poet (1928-)*

CHAPTER 8

Empress Energy

EXTENDING OUR INFLUENCE OUT INTO THE WORLD

*My command stands firm like the mountains and
the sun disk shines and spreads rays over the
titulary of my august person, and my falcon rises
high above the kingly banner unto all eternity.*

*—Hatshepsut, Egyptian Queen/Pharaoh
(1503-1482 BC)*

O nce the Queen has conquered the challenges in Her life, She begins to claim Her royal power. She cuts through fear and ambivalence to become the sole ruler of Her Self. She has struggled for Her transformation and has achieved it. Her proud potency is palpable, Her authenticity uncontested. Her life now takes on a new ease, a grace, a certain lightness of being born of Her Self-knowing, Self-respecting, Self-directing, Self-projecting passion and purpose. She sails ahead on Her own steam, cutting efficiently through seas that are sometimes smooth as glass, sometimes choppy and fraught with danger. Her age and vast experience is Her ballast. She keeps Her center, come what may.

REIGNING SUPREME

But something else remarkable takes place once the Queen has stepped into sovereignty. Now that Her own life is in working order and running more smoothly, the Queen can afford to enlarge the territory and expand the horizons of Her influence and extend the parameters of Her physical, mental, emotional, and spiritual domain. Firmly rooted in Her best Self and acting on Her own behalf, She is free to reach out in ever-increasing concentric circles to others. Now She can freely offer Her compassion, expertise, time, and assistance to the people and causes that call to Her sense of response-ability—literally Her ability to respond. Response-ability is the willingness to encounter each person, situation, event, and emotion with an open heart and an open mind, so that we can respond to the needs of others and our own needs with equal care. Born of awareness and consideration, response-ability means choosing to be fully conscious and present in life and to participate conscientiously in its enfoldment.

In her book, *Women of the 14th Moon*, Brooke Medicine Eagle, a Native American Earth Wisdom teacher, writes, "When our elders step across the threshold of the Grandmother Lodge, leaving their bleeding behind them, they become the Keepers of the Law. No longer is their attention consumed with the creation and rearing of their own family.... Their attention turns to the children of all Our Relations: not just their own children, or the children of their friends, their clan or tribe, but the children of all the hoops: the Two-Leggeds, the Four-Leggeds, the Wingeds, the Finned, the Green-Growing Ones, and all others. Our relationship with this great circle of Life rests ultimately in their hands. They must give away this responsibility by modeling, teaching, and sharing the living of this law—in everyday life—to men, women, children—that all might come into balance."

Maturity brings with it the understanding that everything is not about us. That the world does not revolve around our personal story. That we do not exist in a vacuum. And that all those other people out there actually have lives of their own and are not simply extras in our movie. Life and living have shown the Queen the value of community, cooperation, concern, care, and communion. "Life is the only real counselor," Edith Wharton suggested. "Wisdom unfiltered through personal experience does not become a part of the moral tissue." Knowing Herself to be an integral, inextricably interconnected part of a greater whole, She multiplies Her ministrations to include the welfare of the entire world.

As a woman I have no country.
As a woman I want no country.
As a woman my country is the whole world.
—*Virginia Woolf, English writer (1882-1941)*

ENTER THE EMPRESS

When the Queen assumes Her authority in the ever-greater realms of responsibility and takes it upon Herself to right the wrongs of the world, She ascends to a higher plateau of power. The Empress is the Queen writ large, the level of intensity of Her royal engagement exponentially expanded. Model monarch that She is, the Queen-become-Empress operates from the deep and mighty reserves of Her own personal power and wisdom, wrought through Her dedicated willingness and ability to change, to always, always, change. She is committed to exploring, confronting, and enriching the undeveloped and underutilized parts of Her body, mind, heart, and soul. By working to connect all of the constituent dots of Her many parts, the Queen is constantly becoming ever more of who She truly is—Her Highest Self, Her Extreme Royal Highness, the Empress.

I've found inspiration in numerous wonderful models of the Empress in history, myth, and the wisdom literature from cultures around the world. In the Tarot, the Empress is the Goddess Principle, the Female Cyclical Force that fuels the Universe. Depicted as a mature woman, enthroned upon the twin virtues of wisdom and love, the Empress is the only card in the deck with the heart and the mind in perfect balance.

Cultural anthropologist and educator Angeles Arrien writes, "The Empress represents the trusting balanced heart, rather than the controlling, protective heart. She gives in equal proportion to her capacity to receive and is as comfortable in receiving love as she is in extending love…. She reminds us that *love with wisdom* is the capacity to nurture and support ourselves in equal proportion to how we nurture and support others."

The Empress is sister and ally of the Goddesses of Wisdom in every culture, the mature dispensers of law, order, measure, and balance. Like the Egyptian Isis, the Hellenic Athena, or the Celtic Brigid, the Empress dispenses Her wealth of accumulated wisdom freely, and sides always with what is right, what is honorable, what is helpful, and what is just. She is the creatrix of the world, the nourisher and sustainer of the world. She Herself, in Her body, *is* the world, and we, being part of the world, are part of Her. She is divine, yet She is mortal, residing within each of us as our own inner wisdom.

Empress Wisdom calls us to take part in the life and living of the universe, to take care and precaution, and to take heart. The Egyptian *Book of the Wisdom of Solomon*, written sometime around 100-50 BC in Alexandria, contains the description of a divine female being called Wisdom, or Hochmah, "Though she is but One, she can do all things. And while remaining in herself, she renews all things…. She reaches mightily from one end of the earth to the other. And orders all things well." She works among people to teach us "to know the structure of the world and the activity of the elements, the beginning and end and middle of times, the alteration of the solstices and the changes of the seasons, the cycles of the year and the constellations of the stars, the nature of animals and the tempers of wild beasts, the powers of spirits and the reasonings of humans." In Her great wisdom and largesse, the Empress is ultimately the Guardian of the Good of All.

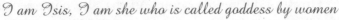

I am Isis, I am she who is called goddess by women
I gave and ordained laws for humans which no one is
  able to change.
I divided the earth from the heavens.
I ordered the course of the sun and the moon.
I appointed to women to bring their infants to birth in
  the tenth month.
I made the beautiful and the shameful to be distinguished
  by nature.
I established punishment for those who practice injustice.
I am the Queen of rivers and winds and sea.
I am in the rays of the sun.
Fate harkens to me.
Hail Egypt that nourishes me.

—From Egyptian Hymn (Second Century)

THE EMPRESS AS LAWGIVER

Like Her forebears in myth and history, the Empress is possessed
of profound thoughts and reasoning abilities. In Egyptian belief, the goddess Ma'at was the All Seeing Eye, Lady of Truth and Right, Goodness and
Judgment. She was named after the term for a measure of land, and Her
particular wisdom is that which gauges, sets standards, illustrates the difference between right and wrong, and ultimately judges the dead as they enter
the underworld with Her scales of justice. On one scale is placed Her symbol, the feather, which represents a lightness of being, ease in the world, a
balance, a respectful harmony with nature. On the other side is placed the
heart of the recently deceased. Measured by Ma'at's scales, only those

whose hearts are as light as Ma'at's feather can attain Heaven.

The Greek Goddess of Wisdom, Athena, also possesses the scales of judgment, dispensing the fate of humankind. With the owl, Her totem animal, perched on Her shoulder, She is the embodiment of Wisdom, Reason, and Purity, the protector of civilized life, law, craft, and agriculture. Even today, the robed Goddess of Wisdom stands outside American courthouses, Her eyes blindfolded to emphasize Her impartial and fair stance, Her scales of justice held aloft for all.

The role of women as dispensers of justice has persisted in the cultures of traditional peoples. Among the Haudenosaunee of the Northeast (called Iroquois by the Europeans), the women had charge of the day-to-day governance of the tribe. The Clan Mothers, post-menopausal wise women, chose the chiefs or council members and held veto power over them, vested with the authority to represent the needs of the people in the discussions and deliberations of the longhouse council.

Popular ombundswomen, they oversaw meetings to prevent abuses of power and to intervene when necessary on behalf of the good of the entire tribe when its collective interests had been ignored. If, in their studied opinion, the chief overstepped his command, the Clan Mothers were empowered to remove his horned helmet. This de-horning signaled that he could not speak for the remainder of that council session, his words rendered meaningless. This practice was the inspiration for the checks and balances system of governance outlined in the United States Constitution, which in turn, was the model for the Charter of the United Nations.

The law of rights and responsibilities of the Clan Mothers is the cornerstone upon which international law is built. Whenever the checks and balances originally written into the working bylaws and rules of government or big business fail, wherever power is wielded irresponsibly, you will find the Empress, a brave mature woman like a Clan Mother, who is willing to speak out in the name of "Truth, Justice, and the American Way." Although the risk to Her personal safety and security is often great, the rock-solid core of Her integrity will allow Her to do no less, consequences be damned. In the face of difficult challenges to the good of the people, the tribal community, the Earth itself, the High Queen Empress rolls up Her sleeves, ties back Her hair, sticks out Her tits, and proposes provocatively, "Make my day!"

THE EMPRESS AS WARRIOR

While the power of the Empress comes from the mature balance of Her passionate heartfelt emotions, and Her clear, calm, reasonable mind, She also embodies the female fighting spirit of the Mother, the lioness, the she-bear, the badger, protecting her young. She is a mighty Amazon-for-right, fierce and unafraid. Her determination-beyond-reason to prevent harm and to prevail in Her rightness is now stabilized by the astute attributes of the Queen. She is a seer, a strategist, a leader, a general who steps back to survey the situation, evaluate the conditions, decide on a strategy, and follow through with a viable plan of action. Athena is not only the Goddess of Wisdom, but also a Warrior Goddess, the protector of towns, and even in war, the consummate Peace Maker. The olive branch is cut from Her holy tree.

When I dare to be powerful—to use my strength
in the service of my vision, then it becomes
less and less important whether I am afraid.
—Audre Lorde, American poet (1934-1992)

The Empress does not usually take up arms to shed human blood. Rather, She turns a terrible face upon the enemies who threaten Her domain from the outside as well as the demons that torment us from within. She deceives and outmaneuvers Her enemies, running them ragged until they can be brought under control. Intimidating them with righteousness, She instills in them a paralyzing fear. Morrigu, the Celtic Goddess of Battle, would take the shape of a mortal woman, and appear before soldiers washing an item of bloodied clothing in a stream. Any warrior seeing Her at Her morbid task would then know that his hours were numbered. In this way, She rendered Her enemies harmless and vulnerable to attack by armies of justice.

Likewise, Kali, the Hindu Goddess of Death, Destruction, and Regeneration, presents an image of dread and horror. Her body smeared red with blood, huge fangs flashing, a tongue dripping fresh blood, She wears a necklace of skulls, earrings of corpses, and is wrapped with writhing snakes as She rides into battle on the back of a lion. Though She is the Goddess of Destruction, what She destroys is marked by sin, ignorance, and decay and gives rise to new life. It is told how Kali fought and killed two demons, and Her devotees believe that Her battle offers an example of how we can defeat our own demons and be free from our debilitating fears.

In Northern European cultures, the Warrior Goddesses are depicted as mature females who are hardly mothering types. Freya, the Great Goddess of the Norse and Teutonic tribes, is the leader of the matriarchs called the Afliae, the Powerful Ones. She is also the Goddess of Love, Beauty, and Sexuality. A true Queen of Her Self, She takes lovers as She will and is in control of Her hot midlife sexuality. Gold and amber are precious to Her, symbolizing Her fiery spirit. She is comfortable with Her fierce nature and refuses to bend to the will of others. A mighty warrior, She rides to battle in Her chariot, but does not usually take part in the fighting Herself. Like Brunihild, the Valkyrie Queen of the *Volsunga Saga*, Her function is to create fear in the hearts of those who would attack Her lands and to inspire Her people to acts of courage.

The Empress is surely the Queen of Fire on fire. She is the flame of passion, of consuming engagement that burns away all that is not in support of life. She is the coal, red-hot, asizzle with Self-directed energy and vigor. She is the coal, white-hot, seething, slow burning, deliberate, patient, and thorough. And She is the ash. What remains when all else is burnt up is the generative source for new life, the mythical Phoenix who rises from the ash to be re-born. She can create and She can destroy.

*Proud Queen of the Earth Gods, Supreme among
the Heaven Gods, Loud Thundering Storm,
you pour your rain over all the lands and all the people.
You make the heavens tremble and the earth quake.
Great Priestess, who can soothe your troubled heart?*

*You flash like lightning over the highlands; you
throw your firebrands across the earth.
Your deafening command, whistling like the South
Wind, splits apart great mountains
You trample the disobedient like a wild bull;
heaven and earth tremble.*

Holy Priestess, who can soothe your troubled heart?

*—Enheduanna, High Priestess of Ur (2300 BC)
A hymn to Inanna, Queen of Heaven and Earth*

EMINENT DOMAIN

As we women, Queens, Empresses, move to assume ever more powerful positions in the world, it behooves us to give careful thought to how we define power. Is power the control wielded by force from an outside source over a person or situation through violence, domination, and repression? Or is power an enabling energy that is generated internally and radiated outward? The Empress emphasizes the careful distinction between aggressive power over, and ennobling power from within—the difference between bully power and authentic power.

Power itself is natural, neutral, whether it is from the sun, the wind, lightning, electricity, geophysical forces, atomic fission, or human charisma. It is the Intention that defines its purpose. To what use is it put? Are its applications beneficial and benign or base and bombastic? Is it a tool for building up or for tearing down? Does it support or suppress the life force? "As long as you keep a person down, some part of you has to be down there to hold him down," counseled the singer Marian Anderson. "So it means you cannot soar as you otherwise might."

Women today have ever-greater access to positions of power, both in our own lives and in the world. We also have more opportunity to draw upon our traditional roles as judges and warriors to speak truth and to monitor power. In recent years we've seen numerous examples of brave Amazon Empresses assuming the role of corporate and governmental whistleblowers—statistically more likely to be women—who dare to call Attention to incidents of irresponsible or devious abuses of power in the interest of the health, welfare, and safety of the public-at-large.

In 2002, *Time* chose as its "Persons of the Year" three remarkable women: FBI Special Agent Colleen Rowley, who had warned the director of the FBI of vital evidence of terrorist activity before the attacks of September 11, 2001, and Sherron Watkins at Enron and Cynthia Cooper at Worldcom, who had uncovered and exposed massive accounting frauds at their respective firms. *Time* celebrated these women as "brave people who did right by just doing their jobs rightly... with the bravery the rest of us always hope we have and may never know if we do."

To add insult to injury, Agent Rowley broke ranks once again when she spoke out in opposition to the War in Iraq and was demoted for her efforts after a twenty-two-year career in the Bureau. Unrepentant and unbowed, the fifty-year-old mother of three has taken her message on the road where she gives speeches about the importance of ethics and ethical leadership. She urges women in the workplace to talk not just about what is best for the bottom line, but to do what is ethically right in any situation as well. Speaking from experience, she warns that such action won't be safe or easy. "But the benefit of behaving ethically and of living in alignment with your values," Rowley promises, "is worth the sacrifice."

I cannot and will not cut my conscience to fit this year's fashions.
—Lillian Hellman, American writer (1905-1984)

Another Empress stepped forward on September 15, 2001, when the Congress of the United States overwhelmingly passed a resolution to give President Bush the authority to use "all necessary and appropriate force" against those whom he deems to be associated with terrorism. The measure passed unanimously in the Senate and by 420 to 1 in the House of Representatives. The sole dissenting vote, "a vote of conscience," as she calls it, was cast was by fifty-three-year-old Barbara Lee, a Democrat from California. "I am convinced that military action will not prevent further acts of international terrorism against the United States," she declared. "There must be some of us who say, 'Let's step back for a moment and think through the implications of our actions today.' Let us more fully understand the consequences." Barbara Lee's spiritual mother, Jeanette Rankin, the first woman elected to the U.S. Congress, was the sole vote in opposition to America's involvement both in World War I in 1917 and World War II in 1941. "You can no more win a war than you can win an earthquake," she told the House of Representatives in casting her vote.

The Hopis say that when the Grandmothers speak, the world will be healed and there will be peace. In February 2003, several Haudenosaunee Clan Mothers, the descendents of those women who so impressed the American founding fathers, issued a public statement to encourage other women to oppose the War in Iraq. "The Americans copied our laws and customs, but they did not understand them," they admonished. "Our way is solving community conflicts through discussion in a People's Council.

In our tradition, three criteria must be kept in mind through all deliberations: Peace: meaning peace must be kept at all costs. Righteousness: meaning decisions must be morally right taking into consideration the needs of seven generations to come. Power: meaning the power of the people must be maintained including the equal sovereignty of all men and women. We are now facing an unnecessary war," their proclamation continues. "We have a duty to use our power to do good. We have decided to remind all humanity of this important truth. War cannot happen without the support of women. We ask the women of the world to come forward and play their rightful role as the progenitors, the creators of all men, of all humanity, the caretakers of the earth and of all that lives upon it."

It is essential to collectively struggle to recover our status as Daughters of the Earth. In that is our strength, and the security, not in the predator, but in the security of our Mother, for our future generations. In that we can insure our security as the Mothers of our Nations.

—Winona LaDuke, Anishinaabekwe (Ojibwe)
    Political activist and Vice Presidential Candidate
    (1959-)

I have found my favorite model of the Empress in the life of an exceptional woman known as Peace Pilgrim who devoted almost thirty years of her life to walking and talking for peace. Born Mildred Norman in 1908, she was in her early forties at the height of the Korean War, the McCarthy Era, and the wholesale international nuclear proliferation with its attendant Ban the Bomb movement. The turmoil in the world around her, no doubt coupled with her own internal changes, caused her to spend a period of concentrated inner questioning about the purpose and direction of her life. Specifically, she wondered what she, one person, could do in the cause of peace. This midlife meditation culminated in her experiencing an intense spiritual awakening, an undeniable epiphany. She came to understand that it was her destiny to become a pilgrim, walking her talk for peace. At the age of forty-five, she gave up all of her possessions—including her name—and prepared to embark upon an incredible pilgrimage that would consume the rest of her life.

On the morning of January 1, 1953, Peace Pilgrim, as she now called herself, set off alone, penniless, without any organized support system, to walk 10,000 miles for peace. She carried her few belongings—a comb, a toothbrush, a pen, and some postage stamps—in the pockets of her tunic. When she left, she pledged to herself in a private vow that she never violated, "I shall remain a wanderer until mankind learns the way of peace, walking until I am given shelter and fasting until I am given food." She shared with everyone she met along her way a printed explanation of her mission that bore the simple message:

This is the way to peace—overcome evil with good,
falsehood with truth, and hatred with love.

During her nearly three decades on the road, she far exceeded her original goal (when she passed the 25,000-mile mark in 1964, she stopped counting). By the time of her death in 1981, Peace Pilgrim had walked across the United States seven times, and had visited ten Canadian provinces and parts of Mexico, spreading her hopeful message of peace and inspiration to the countless thousands of folks who crossed her extraordinary path. Her gentle warrior spirit of wisdom still touches people all over the world through the collection of her writings, *Peace Pilgrim: Her Life and Work in Her Own Words,* which has been translated into twenty-five languages. "To attain inner peace you must actually give your life, not just your possessions," she wrote. "When you at last give your life," bringing into alignment your beliefs and the way you live—then, and only then, can you begin to find inner peace."

THE EMPRESS QUEENS ARE WE

Today, just as the cumulative damage to our Earth is reaching a perilous point of no return and our entire natural and cultural environment is in the throes of dangerous disconnection and dis-ease, we wise, mature, accomplished women are called upon to step up to the challenge and ascend the throne of conscious, conscientious leadership. Rachel Carson, an Empress of the highest order, warned us, "We stand now where two roads diverge. But unlike the roads in Robert Frost's familiar poem, they are not equally fair. The road we have long been traveling is deceptively easy, a smooth superhighway on which we progress with great speed, but at its end lies disaster. The other fork of the road—the one 'less traveled by'— offers our last, our only chance to reach a destination that assures the preservation of the earth."

It is incumbent upon us to use our considerable Queenly power, in whatever way seems appropriate to our individual skills and involvements, to stem the tide of unthinking aggression that can drown us all. In the same way that it was up to us, and only us, to redeem and transform our Selves, we need to grab the reins and redirect and correct the negative and harmful conditions that exist in our community, our society, and our planet.

Daughter of the Goddess I am,
Sister and Mother to my Self.
Queen, Empress, Grandmére Guardian,
Amazon Defender of Right I am.
Protective Nurse to the Earth.
—DH

Once, when I gave a presentation in Washington, D.C. at a conference on the creation of peace in the world and in our lives, I suggested Peace Pilgrim as an inspiring example of an ordinary woman who became an extraordinary peace worker. During the question and answer period, a woman rose and commented that she wished that she, too, could drop her job and just devote her life and herself to peace. "What do you do?" I asked her. "I'm a therapist," she replied. Surely, she has any number of opportunities to help create peace in the lives of those she touches every single day. As does an artist, a teacher, a service employee, a lawyer, a health care provider. Each of us needs to engage in the life and death struggle of Mother Earth in our own unique way and to the best of our experience, special talents, and abilities. The possibility for peace in the world is projected in each smile, each act of compassion, each gift of grace. It is achieved step by small step every day without cease. As the *I Ching* constantly reminds me, "No haste. No rest."

The Empress never gives up hope.

In the same way the Queen creates change for Herself, like the Empress, we can work to effect positive, sane, humane, and sustainable change for the greater good of all. "If we want a free and peaceful world," urged Eleanor Roosevelt, "if we want to make the deserts bloom and man grow to greater dignity as a human being—we can do it." The future we envision starts now, today. And the buck stops here, too, with each of us. To paraphrase Gandhi, we must *be* the future we wish to see. What we seed is what we get. Positive change need not be Earth-shaking or dramatic, nor does it need to be focused only in the political arena. It can be quite personal, subtle, and quiet, yet it does need to be rooted in positive Intention and grown organically with great care and Attention to the purity of the process. The ends do not—cannot—justify the means, because the means have a nasty way of becoming the ends in the end. All we mortals ever have, from moment to moment, is the means. It is our ways and means of thinking and acting that justify our lives.

Despite the ongoing destruction of our environment, I still have a strong feeling of hope for all the creatures on earth.
—Jane Goodall, British primatologist (1934–)

Confident in Her own transformational abilities, the Empress Queen feels that it is Her duty to adopt the lessons that She has learned, the knowledge and understanding that She has gained, and the heady victories She has won, to empower others to rise to their highest potential as well, using Her own life as an example. As Margaret Fuller, the nineteenth-century American Transcendentalist author and editor advised, "If you have knowledge, let others light their candles in it." The Empress Queen is the chief dispenser of order, measure, justice, and right relationship in all realms, Her rule informed by Her keen holistic perspective, as well as the promptings of Her own intuitions. She holds the vision of a world community that is more inclusive, creative, joyful, respectful, and reverential.

The Empress takes a pro-active approach to change.

As She seeks to use the full force of Her personal power as an agent for positive change, the Empress does not turn away from imperfection, nor does She avert Her gaze from the grueling details of life. She opens Her eyes—as well as Her ears—even wider in order to witness, to learn, to help, and to heal. Secure in the knowledge that She can rely safely upon Her instincts and abilities, She opens wide Her heart. Her past losses and pain have taught the Empress Queen to recognize the signs of pain and loss in others—a language She fluently speaks. Comprehending their need, She reaches out to them in sympathy, empathy, advocacy, succor, and support. She does not shrink from Her responsibilities to protect and preserve the very forces of life. The Empress opens Her mouth, as well, and speaks boldly Her truth with the conviction and compassion that commands respect and response.

Our awesome responsibility to ourselves, to our children,
and to the future is to create ourselves in the image of goodness,
because the future depends on the nobility of our imaginings.
—Barbara Grizutti Harrison, American writer
(1935-2002)

It's a big world out there and the plights and problems of humankind can seem insurmountable, impossible to change, but the Empress Queen knows all about change. Has She not been through the rapids of menopause and come out on the other side, altered forever, stronger and smarter by far? A Queen of Her own making, She knows that through effort, patience, and persistence, things can and do improve, that all things are possible. She is the living proof. The Empress does not bite

The Queen Suggests:
Do Something

"So much to do, so little time," you may think. "So many wrongs to right."

And you might well ask, "What can I do? What can just one person do?"

The answer is Do Something.
Do just one simple thing.
You've got to start somewhere.
Start small.

Allot fifteen minutes a day to speak out on issues that are meaningful to you. Make your opinion known. Contact your representatives and urge them to vote in a way as to really represent you. Send emails. Sign petitions. Make phone calls. Write letters to the editor of your local paper. Write checks.

Fifteen minutes a day is definitely doable—just a brief break in your busy schedule. It is possible to accomplish quite a lot in just fifteen minutes. And those short quarter-hours sure add up.

15 minutes a day is almost two hours a week.
15 minutes a day is eight hours a month.
15 minutes a day is sixty hours a year.
15 minutes a day over a year is two and a half days.

Her tongue nor does She withhold Her views. She makes Her beliefs perfectly clear, assumes full response-ability for them, and then takes action to effect change for the betterment of all.

If we, the mighty Empress Queens, bring to bear the amazing experience, understanding, and acumen that we have to share, we can, together, restore balance and bring healing to a world that seems bent on destruction. And we are just the women to do it. Are we not daughters of the Wisdom Goddess? Companions of the Goddess of Protection and Battle? Do we not speak for Her when we step forward in our crowning glory in defense of all life and living? Have we not mastered the art of transformation and positive change, emerging as Queens, Empress rulers by right?

Personally, I do not think that it is a coincidence that just as the planet teeters on the very brink of destruction, there comes along a generation of fiery, accomplished, clever, ambitious women at the height of our supremacy to whip it back into shape. And the sheer enormity of our numbers means that we can actually achieve the critical mass necessary to make a real and lasting difference. Let us harness our impressive Empress Energy: our purity of purpose, our passion, our heartfelt compassion, and our enormous power, and let us direct it toward creating a safe, sublime, and peaceful world for us all. The future is in our very capable hands.

If the first woman God ever made was strong enough to turn the world upside down all alone, together women ought to be able to turn it rightside up again.

—Sojourner Truth, American abolitionist and U.S. General (1797-1883)

For Further Reading

Alcalá, Kathleen. *Women and Aging.* Corvallis: Calyx Books, 1986

Alexander, Lydia Lewis; Harper, Marilyn Hill; Owens, Otis Halloway Patterson; and Lucas, Mildred. *Wearing Purple: Four Longtime Friends Celebrate the Joys and Challenges of Growing Older.* New York: Three Rivers Press, 1996.

Andrews, Lynn V. *Woman at the Edge of Two Worlds: The Spiritual Journey Through Menopause.* New York: Harper Perennial, 1994.

Arrien, Angeles. *The Tarot Handbook: Practical Applications of Ancient Visual Symbols.* New York: Penguin, 1997.

Beckford, Ruth. *Still Groovin': Affirmations for Women in the Second Half of Life.* Naperville, IL: Sourcebooks, Inc., 1999.

Benatovich, Beth, ed.. *What We Know So Far: Wisdom Among Women.* New York: St. Martin's Press, 1995.

Bolen, Jean Shinoda. *Crossing To Avalon: A Woman's Midlife Pilgrimage.* San Francisco: Harper Collins, 1994.

Bolen, Jean Shinoda. *Goddesses in Older Women: Archetypes in Women Over Fifty.* San Francisco: HarperSanFrancisco, 2001.

Borysenko, Joan, Ph.D. *A Woman's Book of Life: The Biology, Psychology, and Spirituality of the Feminine Life Cycle.* New York: Riverhead Books, 1996.

Davis, Elizabeth, and Leonard, Carol. *The Women's Wheel of Life: Thirteen Archetypes of Woman at Her Fullest Power.* New York: Penguin, 1996.

Delany, Sarah L; Delany, Elizabeth A.; and Hearth, Amy Hill. *Having Our Say.* New York: Dell, 1993.

Dowling, Colette. *Red Hot Mamas: Coming into our Own at Fifty.* New York: Bantam, 1996.

Doress-Worters, Paula B., and Siegal, Diana Laskin. *The New Ourselves Growing Older.* New York: Simon and Schuster, 1994.

Drucker, Malka. *White Fire: A Portrait of Women Spiritual Leaders in America.* Woodstock, VT: Skylight Paths Publishing, 2003.

Edelstein, Linda N., Bergen & Garvey. *The Art of Midlife: Courage and Creative Living for Women.* Westport, CT: Greenwood, 1999.

Estes, Clarissa Pinkola. *Women Who Run with the Wolves.* New York: Ballantine, 1992.

Evans, Susan B., Ed.D., and Joan P. Avis, Ph.D. *The Women Who Broke All the Rules– How the Choices of a Generation Changed Our Lives.* Naperville, IL: Sourcebooks, Inc, 1999.

Friedan, Betty. *The Fountain of Age.* New York: Simon & Schuster, 1993.

Gelman, Rita Golden. *Tales of a Female Nomad: Living at Large in the World.* New York: Three Rivers Press, 2001.

George, Demetra, *Mysteries of the Dark Moon: The Healing Power of the Dark Goddess.* San Francisco: HarperSanFrancisco, 1992

Gimbutas, Marija. *The Goddesses and Gods of Old Europe.* Berkeley, CA: University of California Press, 1990.

Greer, Germaine. *The Change.* New York: Knopf, 1992.

Heilbrun, Carolyn. *The Last Gift of Time.* New York: Dial Press, 1997.

Jacobs, Ruth Harriet, Ph.D. *Be an Outrageous Older Woman.* New York: Harper Perennial, 1993.

Jong, Erica. *Fear of Fifty: A Midlife Memoir.* New York: Harper Collins, 1994.

Kaigler, Karen Walker, Ph.D. *Positive Aging.* Berkeley: Conari Press, 1997.

Lessing, Doris. *Summer Before the Dark.* New York: Vintage, 1983.

Lerner, Harriet, Ph.D. *The Dance of Anger: A Woman's Guide to Changing the Patterns of Intimate Relationships.* New York: Harper Perennial, 1997.

MacLaine, Shirley. *Going Within.* New York: Bantam, 1989.

Maier, Mary Anne, and Shaddox Isom, Joan, eds. *The Leap Years: Women Reflect on Change, Loss, and Love.* Boston: Beacon Press, 1999.

Martin, Katherine. *Women of Courage: Inspiring Stories from the Women Who Lived Them.* Novato, CA: New World Library, 1999.

Martz, Sandra Haldeman, and Shere, Deidre. *Threads of Experience.* Watsonville, CA: Papier-Mache, 1996.

McLaine, Patricia. *The Wheel of Destiny.* St. Paul, MN: Llewellyn Publications, 1991.

Monaghan, Patricia. *The New Book of Goddesses and Heroines.* St. Paul, MN: Llewellyn Publications, 1997.

Northrup, Christiane, M.D. *Women's Bodies, Women's Wisdom.* New York: Bantam, 1994.

Painter, Charlotte, and Valois, Pamela. *Gifts of Age.* San Francisco: Chronicle Books, 1985.

Pilgrim, Peace. *Peace Pilgrim: Her Life and Work in Her Own Words.* Santa Fe, NM: Ocean Tree Books, 1982.

Pogrebin, Letty Cottin. *Getting Over Getting Older.* Boston: Little, Brown & Company, 1997.

Porcino, Jane, Ph.D. *Growing Older, Getting Better: A Handbook for Women in the Second Half of Life.* Reading, MA: Addison-Wesley, 1983.

Ransobhoff, Rita M., Ph.D.*Venus After Forty: Sexual Myths, Men's Fantasies, and Truths About Middle Aged Women.* Farr Hills, NJ: New Horizon Press, 1987.

Ridker, Claire, and Savage, Patricia. *Railing Against the Rush of Years.* Hamilton, Ontario, Mekler & Deahl, 1996.

Roundtree, Cathleen. *On Women Turning 50: Celebrating Mid-Life Discoveries.* New York: HarperCollins, 1993.

Rubin, Bonnie Miller. *Fifty on Fifty: Wisdom, Imagination and Reflections on Women's Lives Well Lived.* New York: Warner, 1998.

Sheehy, Gail. *New Passages.* New York: Random House, 1995.

Sheehy, Gail. *The Silent Passage.* New York: Random House, 1991.

Sher, Barbara. *It's Only Too Late if You Don't Start Now: How to Create Your Second Life.* New York: Delacorte, 1998.

Spretnak, Charlene, *The Politics of Women's Spirituality.* New York: Anchor, 1994.

Starhawk. *The Spiral Dance: A Rebirth of the Ancient Religion of the Great Goddess.* San Francisco: HarperSanFrancisco, 1999.

Stasi, Linda, and Rogers, Rosemary. *Boomer Babes: A Woman's Guide to the New Middle Ages.* New York: St. Martin's Griffin, 1998.

Steinem, Gloria. *Revolution from Within: A Book of Self-Esteem.* New York: Little, Brown & Company, 1992.

Taetzsch, Lynne. *Hot Flashes: Women Writers on the Change of Life.* Boston: Faber and Faber, 1995.

Taylor, Dena, and Sumrall, Amber C. *Women of the 14th Moon: Writings on Menopause.* Freedom, CA: The Crossing Press, 1991.

Tenneson, Joyce. *Wise Women: A Celebration of Their Insights, Courage, and Beauty.* New York: Bullfinch Press/Little, Brown and Company, 2002.

Valentis, Mary, Ph.D, and Anne Devane, PhD. *Female Rage: Unlocking Its Secrets, Claiming Its Power.* New York: Carol Southern Books, 1994.

Vickers, Joanne F., Ph.D, and Thomas, Barbara L., M.S.Ed., eds. *No More Frogs, No More Princes: Women Making Creative Choices at Midlife.* Freedom, CA: The Crossing Press, 1993.

Walker, Barbara G. *The Crone.* San Francisco: HarperCollins, 1985.

Walker, Barbara G. *The Woman's Encyclopedia of Myths and Secrets.* New York: HarperCollins, 1983.

Walker, Barbara G. *The Woman's Dictionary of Symbols and Sacred Objects.* New York: HarperCollins, 1988.

Walker, Melissa. *Living on Wilderness Time.* Charlottesville, VA: The University of Virginia Press, 2002.

Weed, Susun. *Wise Woman Ways: Menopausal Years.* Woodstock, NY: Ash Tree Publishing, 1992.

Wilshire, Donna. *Virgin Mother Crone: Myths & Mysteries of the Triple Goddess.* Rochester, VT: Inner Traditions, 1994.

Permissions

Every effort has been made to trace the ownership of all copyrighted material and to secure the necessary permissions to reprint these selections. In the event of any question arising as to the use of any material, the author and the publisher, while expressing regret for any inadvertent error, will be happy to make the necessary correction in future printings.

Grateful acknowledgment is made to the following for permission to reprint excerpts from the copyrighted material listed below:

Canan, Janine. "Dear Body" from *In the Palace of Creation: Selected Works 1969-1999* (Chicago: Scars Publications, 2003). Copyright ©2003 by Janine Canan. Reprinted by permission of the author.

Ethelsdattar, Karen. "Penelope" from *Earthwalking and Other Poems* (Xlibris, 2001). Copyright ©2001 by Karen Ethelsdattar. Reprinted by permission of the author.

Nichols, Grace. "Invitation" from *The Fat Black Woman's Poems* (London: Virago Press, 1984). Reprinted by permission of the publisher.

Rexroth, Kenneth, trans. Li Chi'ing-chao, "A Weary Song to a Slow Sad Tune" from *One Hundred More Poems From the Chinese* (New York: New Directions Publishing Group, 1970). Reprinted by permission of the publisher.

Waters, Geoffrey, trans. Yu Xuanji, "At the End of the Spring" from *A Book of Women Poets From Antiquity to Now*, ed. Willis Barnstone (New York: Schocken, 1962, 1967, 1988). Copyright ©1980 by Geoffrey Waters. Reprinted by permission of the translator.

Wolkstein, Diane, trans. "The Courtship of Inanna & Dumuzi" from *Inanna: Queen of Heaven & Earth, Her Stories and Hymns from Sumer* by Diane Wolkstein and Samuel Noah Kramer (New York: HarperCollins, 1986). Reprinted by permission of the authors.

Wolkstein, Diane, trans. "Loud Thundering Storm" from *Inanna: Queen of Heaven & Earth, Her Stories and Hymns from Sumer* by Diane Wolkstein and Samuel Noah Kramer (New York: HarperCollins, 1986). Reprinted by permission of the authors.

Trinh Thai

Donna Henes is an internationally recognized urban shaman, writer, and artist whose joyful celebrations of celestial events have introduced ancient traditional rituals and contemporary ceremonies to millions of people in more than one hundred cities for thirty years. She is also the author of *The Moon Watcher's Companion, Celestially Auspicious Occasions™: Seasons, Cycles, and Celebrations,* and *Dressing Our Wounds In Warm Clothes,* as well as the CD, *Reverence To Her: Mythology, the Matriarchy, & Me.* In addition to teaching and lecturing worldwide, Mama Donna, as she is affectionately called, publishes an acclaimed quarterly journal, *Always In Season: Living in Sync with the Cycles,* and maintains a ceremonial center, spirit shop, ritual practice and consultancy where she works with individuals, groups, institutions, municipalities and corporations to create meaningful ceremonies for every imaginable occasion.

For further information about Donna Henes's work or to request a calendar of upcoming events, a list of publications and services, and a complimentary copy of *Always In Season,* contact Mama Donna at
www.thequeenofmyself.com